Florida Animals for Everyday Naturalists

SEASIDE PUBLISHING

# Florida Animals

## FOR EVERYDAY NATURALISTS

Larry Allan

Seaside Publishing

Gainesville / Tallahassee / Tampa / Boca Raton

Pensacola / Orlando / Miami / Jacksonville / Ft. Myers / Sarasota

Frontispiece (*top to bottom*): raccoon; white ibis; American alligator

21  20  19  18  17  16    7  6  5  4  3  2

Library of Congress Control Number: 2014937654
ISBN 978-0-942084-46-7

SEASIDE PUBLISHING

Seaside Publishing is a division of the University Press of Florida.

For a complete list of Seaside books, please contact us:
Seaside Publishing
15 Northwest 15th Street
Gainesville, FL 32611-2079
1-352-392-6867
1-800-226-3822
orders@upf.com
www.seasidepublishing.com

For my partner, helper,
and sweetheart, my wife June,
who has contributed so much to my life

•  •  •

# Contents

Preface  ix

## PART III. REPTILES

# Preface

First and foremost, I hope this book proves valuable in moving humankind toward the goal of preserving all wildlife and protecting their natural habitats. It is not meant to provide comprehensive documentation of all wildlife species in Florida. Rather, it selectively presents my personal observations, photographs, and basic facts about some of the mammals, birds, and reptiles I've encountered in the Sunshine State. It pleases me to share with you these wonderful Florida animals.

I've been fascinated by wild animals for a long, long time. And I've been photographing them professionally for more than thirty years. Before that I concentrated my photography on dogs, cats, horses, and birds: people's companion animals. I enjoy the challenges and surprises of trying to capture meaningful photographs and beautiful portraits of wildlife while not interfering with their natural behaviors or giving them reason for alarm due to my presence in their habitats.

After many years of traveling out of our home in San Diego to photograph animals throughout North America, my wife and I realized we had given too little attention to the wildlife of the southeastern United States. To us, that especially meant Florida, which we knew from having visited many times has amazing wildlife diversity.

We moved across the country, settled in, and began to travel and photograph throughout our new home state. This book shows some of the results. We hope you'll enjoy the stories of some of our experiences with Florida's wild animals as they happened. We also hope *Florida Animals for Everyday Naturalists* will answer some of your questions about those encounters.

A number of the animals pictured in this book were photographed in Florida state parks. As an editorial published in the *Ocala Star-Banner* and *Sarasota Herald-Tribune* newspapers announced in 2013, "the real star" of Florida tourism is its "great outdoors. Our woods and waters, our beaches and trails" are what many of the state's millions of annual visitors come expressly "to see and revel in." As a steward of our natural spaces, the Florida Park Service has received three gold medals for excellence from the National Recreation and Park Association, making Florida the only state to receive that award more than once. Plus, our state parks are great places to encounter wildlife.

But Florida state parks are not the only places to meet wild animals. National parks, wildlife refuges and preserves, and county parks abound in Florida to provide you with myriad opportunities to encounter wild animals in their natural habitats.

Thank you for your interest in Florida animals. Our wildlife needs your understanding and your help as well as your admiration. If you are moved to become active in protecting and preserving Florida animals, you might want to consider joining one of the organizations listed in the resources section at the back of the book. I'm sure they will welcome your participation.

Please, do all you can to preserve our wildlife, and help make sure all wild animals have a place to live in freedom, forever.

Part I

# Mammals

# Bobcat

The day was waning. A few last rays of sunshine still bathed the open ground when I spotted the bob-tailed cat moving cautiously over the grass near the road I was traveling. I admired its small ear tufts and tawny coat. Like all wild North American cats, bobcats are solitary animals. This one was indeed alone. Other cars and people on the road did not seem to alarm it at all. Some wild animals get used to having humans nearby.

Bobcats, also known as wildcats, move with such grace and stealth and are a wonder to watch. They rely on keen vision and excellent

A tawny bobcat moves with stealth across the grass within sight of a road.

Though its expression looks rather sweet, the bobcat is also known as a wildcat with good reason.

hearing to hunt. While they use that stealth to stalk their favorite prey, rabbits, they often wait motionless for prey to come close to them, then pounce. In colder climates, like Montana, I've seen bobcat fur frozen in snow where a hungry bobcat waited patiently for a prey animal to wander near.

Bobcats are fairly opportunistic, dining on any small mammal, bird, or reptile, including domestic cats and poultry unfortunate enough to attract their attention.

I've been able to photograph bobcats in spring in Minnesota's greening north woods, in summer among Utah's red rocks, in Canadian forested wilderness areas, in autumn's reds and golds, and in Montana's winter snows. Only found in North America, bobcats inhabit almost all states as well as areas of Canada and Mexico.

Thus it came as no surprise to me that a bobcat was the first wild mammal I saw in Florida on a visit to Myakka River State Park, southeast of Sarasota. Bobcats are the most common wild feline in North America as well as in Florida. They live in almost any type of habitat. And that includes their willingness to accept close proximity to people.

Bobcats den in protected locations, such as a hollow log, under a tree on the ground, or in a rocky shelter or cave. They establish a secluded main or natal den and additional auxiliary or shelter dens in their territories. The latter can be in brush piles, on rock ledges, or even in tree stumps. The nest is made of leaves or other vegetation. It is highly unlikely that a casual hiker would come upon or discover a bobcat den accidentally.

The female bobcat raises her young alone and can have two litters in a year. Kittens are born fully furred but quite helpless. They begin to explore at about one month of age. By two months, they're weaned from mother's milk, but they stay with their mother up to a year. During that time the kittens learn from their mother how to survive on their own.

Of course, the mother will defend her kittens, literally with tooth and claw, as I was reminded on one occasion when I was photo-

Bobcat kittens are protected by tooth and claw!

Bobcat kittens begin to explore at about one month of age, but they still rely on the protection their mother can give them.

graphing a little family in front of their den near a river. The mama bobcat hissed at me, showing her long sharp teeth, then lifted her paw, lethal-looking claws extended, to demonstrate in no uncertain terms that I was being unacceptably intrusive. She hovered over her tiny kittens in her defensive stance. Unfortunately, my long lenses were not long enough to keep me from seeming to threaten the little ones. I backed away quickly but still managed to capture a few images of mama and her little kittens.

The bobcat population in Florida is strong. The cats can be spotted almost anywhere in our state, particularly at night when they are most active. The willingness of the bobcat to live in a variety of habitats and its ability to exist on a wide variety of prey are the reasons this wild cat enjoys a widespread and stable population.

## Bobcat, *Lynx rufus*

Habitat: throughout Florida, including the Everglades; mainly scrub, forests, swamps, and farmlands.

Size: 18–26 inches at the shoulder; 24–42 inches long; 21–38 pounds.

Diet: birds, reptiles, and small mammals, especially rabbits and mice.

Lifespan: up to 15 years in the wild, but generally less than 10 years.

Bobcats' coats turn more gray than brown in winter.

# Florida Panther

In spite of many, many attempts, I have not been able to discover—let alone photograph—a majestic Florida panther in the wild. The tawny cat is an endangered species. The panthers I have photographed are all captives, and that's the way most of us can see these elusive, powerful animals, the largest cats with the ability to purr.

The Florida panther, the state's official animal, is a subspecies of the once extremely widespread big cat known as the cougar, mountain lion, or puma. It is estimated that between 100 and 180 panthers exist in the wild in southwest Florida, an increase from as few as 40–50 individuals near the beginning of the twenty-first century. Introduction of eight genetically close female pumas from West Texas helped correct genetic weaknesses, including sterility, in the Florida population.

Florida panthers are golden-tan, never black. In extreme low light, however, or with sunlight behind them, they may appear darker, which is possibly why early Spanish explorers called the animal a panther, thinking it similar to occasional black leopards from Africa called panthers. Black African panthers, however, are melanistic leopards (a genetic color variation) and not a separate species.

Occasionally, a bobcat is sighted and erroneously labeled a panther by the viewer. The easiest way to tell the difference is the tail. A bobcat's tail is short (bobbed), while a panther's tail is very long (2–3 feet). Panthers can weigh 80 to 154 pounds; bobcats usually weigh less than one-quarter of that.

The U.S. Fish and Wildlife Service (FWS) manages to capture a photo of a wild Florida panther from time to time. Remote automated trail cameras are set up in the Florida Panther National Wild-

Glimpsed with the light at certain angles panthers can appear dark. It's easy to see why early explorers in Florida might have thought this big cat was black, therefore calling it a panther.

All members of the puma species carry their kittens the same way domestic cats do, and they can purr like housecats too.

Though the panther's Latin scientific name means one color, the kittens are multicolored and spotted for protection, making them almost impossible to see as they hide in their dens in palmetto thickets and other protective cover.

life Refuge, located east of Naples, and in other known panther habitats, to capture those images.

FWS reports that fifteen radio-collared females gave birth to forty panther kittens in 2012; nine females gave birth to twenty-one kittens in 2014. Uncollared females give birth to unknown numbers of additional kittens. While Florida records show encouraging growth in panther population, there is, unfortunately, also a marked increase in human population in areas adjacent to panther habitats, which leads to more frequent human-panther interaction. As many as twenty-six free-ranging panthers died in 2012; twenty in 2013. More than half of these 2012 mortalities—seventeen—were caused by "vehicular trauma," the Florida Fish and Wildlife Conservation Commission reports. In 2013 they reported twenty deaths, three-quarters of which were caused by vehicles. Nighttime speed reduction and cautionary road signs are in place, and twenty-four wildlife underpasses have been constructed at known panther crossing sites to allow safe crossings for panthers and other wildlife.

Not all captive Florida panthers feel comfortable with humans nearby, as this one clearly demonstrated when photographed.

People and panthers do not mix comfortably. Interactions will likely increase as human use and development continue to encroach upon panther habitat. Ranchers and other livestock owners have experienced losses due to panther predation. When natural game is abundant, these magnificent big cats are not likely to hunt domestic animals. Panthers must compete with alligators as well as with recently introduced pythons for food.

"With only an estimated 100–160 individuals remaining in the wild, the Florida panther is one of the most endangered mammals in the United States, and the last surviving puma subspecies in the eastern U.S. Though its historic range spanned eight southeastern states, today the panther is restricted to less than 5 percent of its original

This Florida panther is a young female. Panthers are the only puma subspecies now found east of the Mississippi River.

habitat, remaining as a single breeding population in south Florida," the Defenders of Wildlife organization stated in their blog.

The FWS recovery plan for the panther recommends protected habitats for at least 240 panthers each in three viable, self-sustaining populations. The Center for Biological Diversity has twice unsuccessfully petitioned the federal government for the establishment of a second panther population in the Okefenokee National Wildlife Refuge on the Georgia-Florida border.

A male panther needs an estimated 200–300 square miles in order to get enough food to eat. Deer and feral (wild) hogs are favored. Panthers also want to be hidden in a secluded habitat with little or no human contact.

There has never been a reported attack on a human by a Florida panther, though cougars out West have been known to injure or kill people. I hope we can learn to live with our panther population. I am sure I'm not alone in wanting to see and photograph panthers in the wild, as I have the larger puma subspecies in Montana, Utah, California, and parts of Canada.

As with virtually all wildlife species included in this book, volunteers are needed to improve the status of each and every species. The Florida panther is no exception. One group seeking more volunteers to assist with outreach, educational efforts, speaking, fundraising, and general advocacy is Friends of the Florida Panther National Wildlife Refuge. Another organization of volunteers concerned with the survival of the Florida panther is the Florida Panther Society.

With human protection and respect, and ideally with more than a single viable population, Florida panthers should continue to increase in numbers, keeping them at the top of the wildlife hierarchy as the dominant predator in Florida.

Some wildlife conservation and rehabilitation centers have captive Florida panthers from time to time, but they are not necessarily open to the public. Captive Florida panthers can be seen at:

Ellie Schiller Homosassa Springs Wildlife State Park, Homosassa
Lowry Park Zoo, Tampa
Jacksonville Zoo, Jacksonville
Naples Zoo, Naples

The Florida panther's skull shape is different (somewhat flattened) compared to the skulls of other puma subspecies.

## Florida Panther, *Puma concolor coryi*

Habitat: southwest Florida, including the Everglades, Big Cypress National Preserve, and Florida Panther National Wildlife Refuge; mainly forests, swamps, marshland, hardwood hammocks, and palmetto thickets. Habitat loss has severely limited panther populations.

Size: males average 7 feet from nose to tip of tail, 120 pounds; females a little over 6 feet, 82 pounds. One documented male weighed 154 pounds.

Diet: white-tail deer, feral hogs, raccoons, armadillos, rodents, birds, and small alligators; prey usually caught by ambush.

Lifespan: 8–15 years in the wild.

# Foxes

The quick red fox dashed across the road in front of my car as I turned into my neighborhood. I was both delighted and frustrated. This was not the first time I'd seen the shy animal. But previously it had appeared only on the darkest of nights—no good for photography.

Then recently, quite late in the afternoon, I spotted that red fox calmly sitting in the middle of my backyard! At the time I was walking my cat (he's leash trained), so once again there was no opportunity to capture a photograph. The fox scurried quickly away.

Two species of foxes call Florida home: the red and the common gray. The red fox is widely distributed across the northern hemisphere and usually lives in northern Florida, mainly the Panhandle, but it is also found in other parts of the state, including cities, prob-

A red fox has white on its chin and chest.

With great stealth and a long camera lens, you might capture a photograph of a fox sleeping. But any small noise will wake it immediately.

ably having been introduced elsewhere by hunters. Both species are considered cunning and extremely shy.

The red fox's spectacular red coat is easily identifiable, but not all red foxes are red. They can be black, silver, or a mixed pattern called a cross phase, which is reddish-brown with a dark cross on the shoulders. All variations of red fox have a white tip on their very bushy tails.

A gray fox may have a fair amount of reddish-brown fur on its neck, chest, shoulders, lower sides, and the back of the head, in addition to a black streak down the middle of its back. It is therefore often mistakenly identified as a red fox. But only the red fox has a white tip on the tail, clearly identifying this species. The gray fox's natural habitat includes most of the state.

Though a canine, foxes appear catlike. They weigh about what a large domestic cat might weigh—7 to 15 pounds. Gray foxes are the only canine species able to climb trees. They regularly feed, hide, or

The gray fox has red-brown fur on the back of its head and shoulders, plus some white on the chest.

This young red fox, called a kit, is about eight weeks old.

rest in trees. Sometimes called "tree foxes," they use the long claws on their hind legs to dig into the tree's bark. They also stalk their prey in a catlike manner.

Foxes are nocturnal but may occasionally be seen out and about near dawn and dusk. I've been lucky enough to find and photograph them in daylight, including asleep. Only long lenses and great stealth could allow me that opportunity. A fox's hearing is so acute that it can hear small prey digging, gnawing, or rustling underground.

Foxes are among the wildlife species in Florida relying on gopher tortoises and armadillos, enlarging their burrows for the fox's own dens. Young foxes are often taken by raptors (birds of prey) and coyotes. Adult foxes are prey for bobcats and dogs. In turn, foxes help reduce populations of rabbits, mice, and rats.

But humans have now introduced a problem for the mammals and birds that feed on rodents—highly toxic poisons, used especially on rats. These are very effective anticoagulant rodenticides, but the poisons continue to work on any animals eating the poisoned rodents, killing them as well. Wildlife considered desirable to humans has thus become unnecessary collateral damage from these second-generation anticoagulant poisons.

## Red Fox, *Vulpes vulpes*

Habitat: upland fields and pastures (not wooded areas).

Size: 10–16 inches tall at the shoulder; 10–15 pounds; 2–3½ feet long, plus a 1–1½-foot bushy, white-tipped tail.

Diet: rabbits, mice, and rats. The red fox will cache (hide) food for another day when it has eaten its fill.

Lifespan: up to 15 years, but 2–4 years in the wild on average.

• • •

## Gray Fox, *Urocyon cinereoargenteus*

Habitat: throughout Florida, though more plentiful in the north, favoring wooded wilderness areas and inaccessible cover.

Size: 14–15 inches tall at the shoulder; 7–13 pounds; 40 inches long, including a bushy, black-tipped tail at least 1 foot long.

Diet: varied—mice, rats, rabbits, birds, reptiles, amphibians, fish, fruit, berries, insects.

Lifespan: 4–10 years in the wild; up to 15 years maximum.

# Coyote

Florida's wild canids include the coyote. Several times I've seen these shy, elusive animals crossing roads or skirting me in fields with their tip-toe gait, keeping a wary eye on my movements. They're highly adaptable and can be found in all sorts of habitats, with the possible exception of sawgrass areas in the Everglades.

Coyotes have not always been native to our state, but they began expanding their range in the Southeast in the 1960s and have been increasing their numbers in Florida since the 1970s. Most frequently

Coyotes, intelligent and adaptable canines, stalk and then pounce on their prey.

Sometimes coyotes seem to howl just for the sheer joy of it.

seen in our northern counties, coyotes have now reportedly been seen in all Florida counties, including in urban areas.

I have watched them instructing their pups in the art of hunting in the open fields they prefer. They're skilled hunters with excellent sight, hearing, and sense of smell. Both parents help raise and teach the youngsters. However, coyotes are not true pack animals, like wolves, just strongly family oriented.

Early one morning I watched an adult coyote, trailed by two pups, stalk and pounce on a field mouse with a flying leap. Then it released the startled little mouse to encourage a hunting response from the two youngsters that were watching carefully. And the adult coyote went through the lesson all over again, with what seemed to be parental affection.

Enlarged gopher tortoise or armadillo burrows often serve as dens for a litter of coyote pups. And a breeding pair might return to those usurped burrows again and again for succeeding litters.

The Latin name for the coyote translates as "barking dog." They are well known for their howls, yips, and barking vocalizations, both

A coyote pup nips at the mouth of its parent, hoping the adult will regurgitate some food after a morning's hunt.

singly and as a group exercise, most likely to be seen or heard near dawn or dusk. Coyotes are basically crepuscular; that is, primarily active at dawn and dusk. However, they may be seen at almost any time of day or night.

Occasionally gray foxes are mistakenly identified as coyotes. Both species have bushy tails, though the fox easily wins that competition. Coyotes carry their tails low when running; foxes tend to carry their tails straight back when running, and dogs' tails generally are carried in an upright position. Coyotes are larger than foxes, and they are the fastest of all wild canine runners. Coyotes generally run at 25–30 miles per hour but can reach 40 mph.

While coyotes do not represent a physical threat to humans, people must be careful not to encourage coyotes with careless behavior. Small children or pets should not be left unattended in yards; pet

Coyotes run with their tails down, unlike other canines.

A very young coyote cautiously leaves its den to explore.

food should not be left outdoors at night; and garbage containers should be secured carefully to avoid opportunistic scavenging coyotes (and other species, such as black bears). Coyotes can live very successfully near humans due to our own careless ways.

Coyotes are perhaps the ultimate survival specialists. Most assuredly, they've carved out a place in Florida's natural ecosystem.

## Coyote, *Canis latrans*

Habitat: varied—open fields, farmland, scrub, forests.

Size: 23–26 inches at the shoulder; 3½–4½ feet long, plus a black-tipped tail of 12–15 inches; 20–35 pounds.

Diet: opportunistic and omnivorous—rats, mice, rabbits, birds, insects, fruit, carrion.

Lifespan: 6–8 years in the wild on average; one was reported to live to age 14 in the wild.

A coyote speaks.

# White-Tailed Deer

Over the years my work as an animal photographer has taken me to places in North America where species strong, wise, and untamed come together. Like grizzly bears and bald eagles in Alaska, for instance. Or like mountain lions and gray wolves in northwestern Montana. And like American alligators and great blue herons in southern Florida.

But it is not always the large, aggressive, or spectacular species that make the biggest impression. Sometimes it's the unique encounters with common wildlife I remember the most.

My wife and I were on a country walk with our three dogs in Manatee County one lovely spring day. We followed a little path worn in the brushy undergrowth through a wooded area. The dogs led the way.

To our surprise, our dogs scampered right past a white-tailed deer fawn lying motionless near a bush close to the path we trod—within less than six feet, I'm sure. My wife and I both saw the fawn, but none of the dogs took any notice of the young creature lying there so close to us. With eyes wide open in fright, it did not move.

That behavior—or lack of it—made me wonder. And so I began to research deer and their actions or reactions.

First, I learned that a deer fawn does not have an odor. The dogs couldn't sniff out the nearby fawn because it did not give off any scent. This is one of nature's ways of protecting the little ones. Those spots on their coats, which fade at about three to four months of age, make it difficult to see them. That's another defense mechanism nature provides them.

The most important thing I learned about deer is that a fawn is

A white-tailed deer doe is trailed by her fawn in Myakka River State Park.

This white-tailed deer fawn did not move an inch as my three dogs raced right by it. Remaining perfectly still was its way of staying out of sight.

left by its mother when the adult doe goes off to feed. And the fawn stays right where mama leaves it. That way the parent has no trouble returning to the youngster. Nor does the doe call the attention of a possible predator to the fawn by the presence of the doe's own scent. It is not unusual to find a fawn curled up in the woods, peacefully napping while it awaits its mother's return.

There is an important message here. If you should come upon a deer fawn apparently abandoned in the woods, do not assume the animal is an orphan. The fawn is much more likely to be waiting for its mother's return right to where she left it when she went off to forage.

Deer are found everywhere in Florida, especially in old long-leaf pine forests. They're also found throughout the United States and along the southern border areas of Canada. A fawn stays with its mother about a year.

Cutting forests and clearing land has actually aided the white-tailed

Found only in the Florida Keys, diminutive key deer are a subspecies of white-tailed deer.

Loss of caution about humans and traffic enables key deer to feed comfortably right beside roads in the Keys.

deer population. White-tailed deer are plentiful now and rank as the most populous hoofed mammal in America. Hunting restrictions and the great reduction in the numbers of its natural predators—wolves, mountain lions, and, in Florida, Florida panthers—have also aided their population increase. Deer are the panther's favored prey.

The white tail of this species is important. When alarmed, deer raise their tails as a signal to others, known as flashing white. For prey animals like deer, flight is the key response when frightened. The white flash makes it easier for a fawn to follow its mother in swift escape.

Groups of white-tails are seldom seen, though a doe might be followed by one or two fawns. Only the males grow antlers. Bucks begin to grow antlers a few months after birth and shed them annually, with the antlers growing additional points as the bucks mature. The size of a buck's antlers is not solely a function of age. Antler size is also determined by the quality of nutrition the animal receives. Our Florida deer tend to be smaller than northern subspecies because sandy soil has fewer nutrients. Plants deer eat in Florida therefore provide less nutrition.

Primarily active and foraging at dawn and dusk (that is, crepuscular), white-tailed deer generally bed down during daylight hours to digest their food in an area providing concealment, but you might see them moving to feeding areas along established trails at any time. They move with grace, can run at up to 35 miles per hour, and can clear an eight-foot fence with ease. They're also strong swimmers.

There are three subspecies of white-tailed deer in Florida. The Florida coastal white-tail is generally found in the Panhandle; the Florida white-tail occurs in the Florida peninsula; and the diminutive and endangered key deer is found principally on Big Pine Key and No Name Key. There are only about one thousand key deer.

I always enjoy seeing deer—even without a camera in my hand. They are beautiful creatures to watch.

### White-Tailed Deer, *Odocoileus virginianus*

Habitat: throughout Florida, including the Everglades; mainly brush, woods, open grassland, farmlands, even home gardens.

Size: males average 125 pounds, females 95 pounds; 24–36 inches tall.

Diet: leaves, tips of woody shrubs, vines, succulents, grasses, acorns, mushrooms, aquatic plants.

Lifespan: up to 20 years; average is 6 years due to mortality from hunting.

• • •

### Key Deer, *Odocoileus virginianus clavium*

Habitat: National Key Deer Refuge, basically Big Pine Key and No Name Key. Shelters in pine forests, hardwood hammocks, freshwater wetlands, and mangrove swamps.

Size: 55–80 pounds; 27 inches tall; does smaller than bucks.

Diet: mangrove trees, thatch palm berries, roadside grasses, garden plants.

Lifespan: males about 3 years; females 5–6 years.

# Raccoon

As we sat at the picnic table in Sarasota's South Lido Key Park, my wife felt a soft tap-tap-tap on the back of her ankle. She looked down and discovered a masked face looking up at her with what she could only describe as a pleading expression. Behind the mama raccoon sat a coterie of her four youngsters (kits), watching cautiously.

It was difficult not to give in to that sweet, pleading little animal. However, we knew it was not in the wild creature's best interests to feed it. "No. No," my wife said to them in a stern voice. They moved away. We knew that feeding bears, foxes, and raccoons is a crime in Florida. These animals are not pets. For the health and well-being of

Look into the irresistible eyes of a raccoon. Raccoons are among the most commonly seen wildlife in Florida, willing to live close to people and sometimes regarded as pests.

Raccoons prefer to live where trees are nearby—for safety and for nesting.

both raccoons and humans, we must not treat raccoons as if they are domesticated.

Raccoons, often simply called coons, are among the most common of all wild animals, not just in Florida but throughout North and Central America. They have become especially successful in living alongside humans, including in urban areas. Adaptable animals, they simply require areas with trees nearby, where they nest in hollows. Trees also make a safe place for raccoons to sleep during daylight hours. Raccoons can come down a tree head first since they have the ability to rotate their hind feet 180 degrees.

One caution about raccoons: they are known carriers of rabies, distemper, and tuberculosis, though the incidence of these diseases is not startlingly high. They can pass disease to any pets that are not vaccinated.

Though classified by biologists as carnivores, raccoons eat almost

Raccoons use their dexterous forepaws like hands when feeding.

anything and everything—including fruits, nuts, and seeds. We had one neighborhood raccoon that consistently raided one of our bird feeders at night.

Raccoon predators include dogs, Florida panthers, bobcats, great horned owls, and alligators. Alligators actually provide protection for bird nests and roosting birds by preying on the raccoons that prey on eggs and sleeping birds in nests.

The Florida Keys have a subspecies of raccoon that is unique. It is smaller, has a different shape (less bearlike), and has a different color and coat but retains the well-known bandit's mask and ringed tail.

Although many people consider raccoons a nocturnal pest, I enjoy

"No. No," we sternly told the raccoons. And they moved away.

Young raccoon kits look out from the safety of a cavity in a downed tree.

This raccoon seemed to be looking at us with a pleading expression in Sarasota's South Lido Key Park.

watching them with their gentle ways and disarmingly cute appearance. But it is important for us to remember not to encourage them to move right in with us, which they seem almost willing to do.

### Common Raccoon, *Procyon lotor*

Habitat: throughout Florida, including urban areas.

Size: 10–15 pounds; 2–3 feet long including a ringed tail of about 10 inches; about the size of a cat or small dog, but larger—up to 30 pounds in northern states.

Diet: opportunistic and omnivorous rather than carnivorous—fruits, nuts, seeds, vegetable matter, roots, grapes, sea grapes, pawpaws, cabbage palms, saw palmetto, cactus, acorns; amphibians, reptiles, birds, fish, insects, eggs (bird and reptile); garbage.

Lifespan: 2–3 years.

# Gray Squirrel

Though Florida has three species of squirrels, we are most likely to see the eastern gray rather than the larger fox squirrel or the southern flying squirrel. And I must admit, every time I spend a few minutes watching one of these busy little creatures in my yard (where two of

This eastern gray squirrel scampers along a fallen log.

them reside) or in fields or forests I might be tramping, I grow a smile at their antics.

Like so many of us, the eastern gray squirrel is mostly an urban and suburban dweller, though the species was originally a forest dweller. Of course, it wants trees. That's where it chooses to nest, in tree hollows or in nests constructed of dead leaves and twigs and lined with fur or feathers. These nests are called dreys and are larger than many bird nests. Gray squirrels also take to the trees to avoid danger whenever they feel threatened.

Sitting up for a better look around, this eastern gray squirrel in Myakka River State Park is calmly alert.

Squirrels can rotate their back legs 180 degrees to assist their quick descent down a tree.

Oh, yes, and squirrels will also nest in chimneys, attics, and the walls of buildings.

Found throughout Florida, the eastern gray squirrel chatters when disturbed. This squirrel is a strong swimmer, probably part of the reason it's so widespread in our state. I've seen one leap into a pool to flee from a human, and I've seen them swimming in small bodies of water in doglike fashion, head held up at a slight angle and back above the water's surface.

Two formidable predators—hawks and crows—hunt gray squirrels, but we know there is no present danger to their large population. However, too many squirrels can lead to the destruction of crops, electric wiring, wood, plastic, and more. Squirrels are rodents, and one of the things that distinguishes rodents is that their teeth are constantly growing. Therefore rodents must continuously gnaw on things to grind down their teeth. They face potential starvation when their teeth get too long to function correctly.

One fascinating thing I love to watch is their quick, head-first dash down a tree or down the screens surrounding our lanai. How can they do that? Their back feet can rotate 180 degrees, allowing their rear claws to hook firmly into a tree's bark or into a screen.

Squirrels are perhaps best known for their very bushy tails. That magnificent tail is used for balance on a dash through trees, as a shield when its owner is in battle, or for warmth on cold nights in winter.

When I was a boy in Minnesota, I occasionally fed nuts to a gray squirrel in our backyard. I didn't know any better when I was ten. Now I do. Each spring for several years, that little mama squirrel would bring around her new litter of little ones. I was delighted that she seemed to want to share her good news with me. Unhappily for me, my parents moved to another city. I missed my little gray friend, but I hoped she continued to live and have lovely families without any nutritional assistance from me—just as the normal and natural pattern had been for squirrels forever.

### Eastern Gray Squirrel, *Sciurus carolinensis*

Habitat: woodlands as well as suburban and urban areas.

Size: 15 or more inches with 7½ to 9-inch tail; about 1 pound.

Diet: omnivorous—nuts, including acorns; fruits, including grapes, tupelo fruit, and berries; seeds, including cypress and elm seeds; insects, bird eggs, and more.

Lifespan: approximately 6 years.

# Striped Skunk

My neighbor's teenage son walked onto our porch with his new pet—a striped skunk. I was surprised and somewhat tentative. It smelled a bit musky but not overpoweringly. He told me his young skunk had been de-scented. The small animal seemed to be content to be held in the boy's arms and gently stroked.

There is a busy trade in pet skunks in Florida. However, my interest is in the ones that are truly wild, living in their natural habitat.

Almost everyone knows what a skunk looks like. Florida, however, boasts two species—striped and spotted. Both are about the

Double trouble? This pair of young wild striped skunks can already spray effectively.

A baby striped skunk enjoys our front garden. Is it searching for insects or simply enjoying the sweet floral scents?

size of a house cat, though with small heads. Both are black animals with white markings, and both carry that ultimate defensive weapon, musk glands near the anus under a bushy tail. They can effectively spray about 15 feet, though small droplets of the discharge may carry up to three times that far in the air. And both species are nocturnal omnivores. Their lack of any camouflage is a clear warning to all that they are animals to be avoided.

Skunks are prey for dogs, coyotes, foxes, and bobcats. Their most successful predator is the great horned owl.

Though perfectly able to dig, skunks seem to prefer to occupy abandoned armadillo and gopher tortoise burrows to raise their young. They also den in piles of wood or brush and in tall grassy areas.

At one time we had a cat-safe fenced-in yard. One of our cats came into the house one evening after dark crying loudly and reeking of a scent that could only have come from a skunk. He was obviously in pain, frantically wiping at his eyes with his paws. His beautiful blue eyes were squinting, tinted red, and highly irritated.

A mature wild striped skunk ambles through the grass.

Normally, skunks give several warnings before they spray. A striped skunk will face its adversary, arch its back, lift its tail with tail hairs bristling, click its teeth in a chatter, and stomp its front feet on the ground before turning its body around to lift the tail straight up and spray. I have no idea how many of these movements our cat saw before that ultimate moment, but he obviously did not get the skunk's message.

I immediately took him into a bathtub for treatment. While there are commercially available products on the market for this purpose, we didn't have any on hand. I relied on plain tepid water to rinse out the cat's eyes, used a no-more-tears type baby shampoo on the head and near his eyes, and employed a mixture of 3 percent hydrogen peroxide, liquid soap (dishwashing liquid), and baking soda to treat the rest of him. The exact formula is available on the Internet.

Our cat was available to meet friends again in just two or three days. We had to make the yard skunk-proof, too. It was strange that skunks could get in, but our cats could not get out. But I certainly didn't want to have our cat suffer another painful and undignified assault.

I did miss seeing those striped visitors from time to time. Their diet—including beetles and their larvae, crickets, grasshoppers, and other garden pests—helped us maintain healthy plantings. And I especially missed seeing, from time to time, the cute four to seven little ones trailing behind their mother through our yard.

## Striped Skunk, *Mephitis mephitis*

Habitat: throughout Florida, except the Keys; mainly brush, pasture, and residential areas.

Size: 23–31 inches with a 7–15-inch tail; average weight a little over 7 pounds.

Diet: small mammals, bird eggs, amphibians, insects in lawns, fruit trees and garden plants, roots, seeds, and more.

Lifespan: 2–3 years in the wild; pets about 5 years.

# Black Bear

As we rolled to a stop behind a line of other cars, I stretched to see why traffic on a state route east of Ocala had halted in both directions.

There, to my surprise, standing tall like a traffic cop in the middle of the road, was one irate mama black bear. She looked as if she would brook no nonsense from anyone as she established a safe path for her two little cubs to cross the busy road. She had stationed herself exactly in the center of the road and stretched upward to her full height—a bit more than six feet, I guesstimated. Her eyes could only

This black bear has the shiny black coat and brown fur on its nose that easily identify the species.

Florida's black bears are an adaptable subspecies.

be described as glaring at the motionless vehicles, seemingly promising big trouble to any motorist foolish enough to test her authority. It is best not to fool with a mama bear.

Once she had established a safe path for the cubs to cross, she called the two babies waiting dutifully at the side of the road. Mama bear stood sentry until both cubs were safely across. Only then did she abandon her combative stance and shuffle off the road, allowing traffic to resume. The little family of three ambled off into the woods on the other side.

No, I did not have a camera with me that day.

The Florida black bear is an adaptable subspecies of the black bear found in much of North America. Its shiny black coat and brown muzzle readily identify it—however, not all black bears are black. Some are brown, and in the western United States they can be cinnamon. Others are so light-colored as to be virtually white or silvery gray (known as glacier bears or spirit bears), though these are not found in Florida but only in British Columbia, Canada, and southeastern Alaska.

The largest terrestrial or land animal found in Florida, black bears are the only species of bear extant here. The other two North American bears are the much larger grizzly or Alaskan brown bear and the polar bear.

Black bears are solitary except at breeding times. Like other bears, they hibernate. Because our climate is what it is, Florida bears may

Black bears walk on their full foot (like humans) rather than on their toes as many other four-footed mammals do.

Not all black bears are black.

leave hibernation from time to time to forage, and some bears in Florida do not hibernate at all. However, expectant mothers must hibernate. They tend to hole up from December to about April to give birth to their young.

In order to accommodate hibernation, bears bulk up in the autumn, eating four or five times their usual amount of food. Black bears are omnivores, and about 80 percent of their diet is plant based—fruit, nuts, berries, and even the plants themselves (for fiber).

Honey is a well-known favorite food of bears. Not only do black bears love the sweet sticky stuff, but they also eat the larvae they find in beehives (for protein).

There are eight areas within the state that have bear populations. They include Big Cypress in southwestern Florida; Osceola in the northeastern border area; St. Johns, also in the northeast region, which provides desirable contiguous wetlands and upland habitats; Ocala in central Florida; and Appalachicola and Eglin, both in the Panhandle area. Generally speaking, the population of bears in Florida is stable. They were taken off the list of threatened wildlife by the Florida Fish and Wildlife Conservation Commission in 2012. Hunting bears in Florida is against the law. The number one cause of bear

A Florida black bear ambles along a fence near Ocala National Forest.

A black bear cub is learning by tasting.

deaths (about 90 percent) is encounters with vehicles. Roadkill is an awful way to lose one of these wonderful, shy animals.

Bears usually want to get away from people, as do most other wild animals with which I've come in contact. Our black bears are not ferocious, but they have been known to bite or scratch people.

Black bears have excellent vision and sharp noses with a good sense of smell. Though their gait is most often a shuffle, they can run in excess of 30 miles per hour for short distances. Bears are also good swimmers. They are crepuscular—primarily active at dawn and dusk. At these times of day a driver's vision is at its worst, which explains the high numbers of vehicular deaths suffered by bears. Please remember to slow down your vehicle at dawn and dusk, for the benefit of both humans and wildlife. Give 'em a "brake."

One other source of problems between humans and bears involves easy access to garbage and other food that we may inadvertently leave out for them. Bears raid garbage and pet food containers, such as dog dishes left outside and bird feeders. Once bears associate getting food with humans, they lose their fear of our species, and that creates dangerous human-animal interactions. All too often, these encounters lead to the death of a "nuisance bear" at human hands. Please avoid teaching bears or other wildlife to depend on us.

A few simple precautions can prevent unnecessary deaths of wild animals. The state Fish and Wildlife Commission and several organizations, like Defenders of Wildlife, have information available on the Web to help us avoid these tragedies by bear-proofing our property.

### Black Bear, *Ursus americanus floridanus*

Habitat: varied, most of Florida in oak, pine, and scrubby upland hardwood forests; some wetlands. Habitat reduction has limited this species' population.

Size: males 250–400 pounds (600 pounds possible), females 125–250 pounds; 4–6 feet long; 2½–3½ feet tall at the shoulder.

Diet: omnivorous—mostly vegetation, including saw palmetto, corn, persimmon, nuts, fruits and berries; insects, crayfish, turtles, alligator and bird eggs, small animals of various kinds; honey; human garbage.

Lifespan: up to 24 years.

# Dolphins

Dolphins are readily seen along the shores of Florida. They lazily swim the coastlines, not far offshore from where we might be swimming or fishing. They play in the wakes of boats. And they're on display as captives at several locations around the state, including Orlando, Miami, St. Augustine area, Clearwater, and the Keys. The movies *Dolphin Tale* and *Dolphin Tale 2* were photographed in part at the Clearwater Marine Aquarium.

The bottlenose dolphin is the species most often seen in Florida waters. However, in deeper Gulf of Mexico waters pantropical spotted dolphins can be observed. It is difficult to tell the difference be-

Bottlenose dolphins are the most frequently seen species in Florida waters.

tween these two species when we see them in the wild. The pantropical spotted dolphin has a longer, more slender beak than does the bottlenose, but the spots can be hard to see. Newborn calves do not have spots. They develop later.

Cruising up the Intracoastal Waterway near Midnight Pass in Sarasota County, our son's boat was visited by a bottlenose dolphin swimming alongside us, tilting its head so that its mouth was visible to us. It was begging for food. Many people, delighted to see a wild dolphin so close at hand, had dropped bites of food to it for more than twenty years. The behavior of begging was totally ingrained in this individual. Boaters who knew him well called him "Beggar." Slapping the side of the boat would bring him over.

I'm sorry to tell you Beggar was recently found floating in the water, dead. Scientists then had a chance to examine him closely. He was 25–35 years old and definitely underweight and dehydrated. It seems Beggar had given up normal dolphin pursuits for a way of life that

Powerful and intelligent, bottlenose dolphins appear to be happy creatures, but the "smile" is not a reflection of their feelings—it's simply the way they're formed.

Nicknamed "Beggar," this bottlenose dolphin swam from boat to boat seeking food. He suffered greatly from his own success.

caused him to be below average in weight and shortened his lifespan dramatically too. Male dolphins normally live up to fifty years in the wild.

Beggar's behavior put him at high risk of being struck by boats. His body showed that he had both healed scars and healed broken bones, most likely caused by boat strikes. He was also known to bite people who tried to pet him. Do not be misled by their gentle-seeming behavior. Dolphins can be aggressive.

It was documented that Beggar had been fed beer, hot dogs, pretzels, candy bars, chips, and cookies. He had squid beaks (not normal prey for dolphins here), fish hooks, and fishing line in his stomach. The Marine Mammal Protection Act makes it illegal to feed wild dolphins and to harass them. Was Beggar killed with kindness? Though it appears so, he was actually killed by a lack of human understanding.

Powerful and intelligent, dolphins captivate humans. It has recently been reported, for example, that dolphins call each other by "signature whistles," which act as names of individuals, and they respond by repeating these when they hear the sound of their own signature whistle. And it seems that humans are interesting to dolphins too.

These marine mammals are known to be cooperative hunters, and they're very vocal. They produce both whistles and clicks. The clicks are not communicative but rather work like sonar to help dolphins locate food, avoid predators, and navigate the oceans.

Many captive dolphins are confined in relatively small tanks. These marine mammals stop utilizing their natural radarlike echo-location ability because of the cacophony of sounds pinging back to them from circular tanks. They are often subjected to chemically treated artificial salt water, too, according to Ric O'Barry's Dolphin Project. He's a leading activist for dolphins and author of *Behind the Dolphin Smile*. O'Barry emphatically points out these are two reasons dolphins should not be kept in captivity.

It is great fun to watch dolphins swimming effortlessly, diving, jumping vertically into the air with abandon, and riding a boat's bow waves powered by those strong tail flukes—all the while exhibiting that great dolphin smile. In reaction, most of us can't help but smile too.

A pantropical spotted dolphin recuperates at Mote Marine Laboratory in Sarasota. This species inhabits deeper waters in the Gulf of Mexico than does the bottlenose dolphin. The crease across its forehead is a natural characteristic of the species.

My smile turned to a deep frown, however, when I learned that up to 54 dolphins, over 100 manatees, and some 300 pelicans died in the Indian River Lagoon on Florida's east coast in early 2013. Biologists are scrambling to discover the exact cause or causes, but pollution from nutrients and fertilizer runoff are suspected of fueling exceptionally huge algal blooms. Sea grass beds, the basic food of manatees, were killed off there in 2011. The lagoon is a 156-mile-long estuary representing about 40 percent of Florida's Atlantic coast. Let us hope the mystery will be solved soon, and these important species will be saved from further devastation.

### Bottlenose Dolphin, *Tursiops truncatus*

Habitat: inshore and offshore waters.

Size: 6–12 feet long; 310–1,450 pounds, though not this heavy in Florida waters.

Diet: fish—especially pinfish, sheepshead, flounder, mullet—and some invertebrates; can eat 20 pounds per day.

Lifespan: more than 50 years.

• • •

### Pantropical Spotted Dolphin, *Stenella attenuata*

Habitat: tropical and warm-temperate seas around the world. In the Gulf of Mexico, offshore waters are preferred.

Size: a little over 8 feet long; about 265 pounds.

Diet: small fish including flying fish and mackerel, shrimp and other crustaceans, squid.

Lifespan: approximately 40 years.

# Manatee

During our first winter in Florida, my wife and I drove to Crystal Springs to see the unique animals scientists labeled sirenians. They're the source of legends about lonesome sailors mistaking them for mermaids or sea nymphs and of Greek myths about sirens whose singing lured ships to destruction on rocky shores.

After seeing manatees, I cannot understand how such myths could have started. These marvelous animals are bewhiskered, slow-moving eating machines measuring an average of nine or ten feet long and weighing upward of 1,000 pounds—not quite the picture that comes to my mind for a sea nymph!

A captive manatee feeds at the water's surface in Ellie Schiller Homosassa Springs Wildlife State Park.

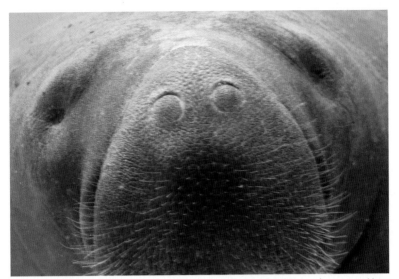

The manatee's whiskers are sensory organs to help find food in murky waters. Note the tightly closed nostrils.

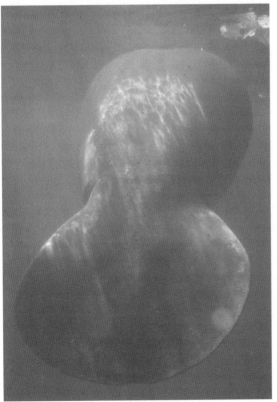

A manatee's tail is rounded and propels the marine mammal with an up-and-down motion. Fish swim with a side-to-side motion of their tails.

As the waters around Florida cool during the winter months, manatees seek warm springs or the warm effluent of industrial plants, such as a power company's electricity-generating plant, to escape the cold. There are twenty-four such warm water sources around the state, six of which are natural springs. Crystal River has one of those natural springs, which serves as a gathering place for manatees. Although cold weather caused the deaths of more than four hundred manatees in just two years (2010–11) due to hypothermia, boat strikes cause an even greater number of manatee fatalities.

The oldest known manatee celebrated its sixty-fifth birthday in 2013. Snooty is on display at the South Florida Museum in Bradenton and can be viewed from both above and below the water's surface. The museum also provides rehabilitation for sick or injured manatees to prepare them for release back into the wild.

Technically, the species name is West Indian manatee. It is listed as an endangered species, but a movement backed by recreational boaters and others wants federal officials to adjust that listing to threatened.

Manatees can reach 13 feet in length and weights of over 3,500 pounds. Their flippers are paddle shaped for swimming but can also be used to grasp vegetation to eat. Their tails are rounded and propel them through water with an up-and-down motion. This same locomotion is seen in other marine mammals, such as dolphins and whales.

Their whiskers are sensitive, assisting them in finding food during approximately eight hours per day of grazing. They have only six neck vertebrae (most mammals have seven), resulting in an inability to turn their heads. A manatee must turn its entire body around to look back.

Manatees, also called sea cows, can hold their breath for up to twenty minutes, though they normally come up for a breath of air every three or four minutes. When they come up to breathe, usually only the nostrils are above water. Underwater they can close their nostrils tightly. They also have a nictitating membrane able to protect their eyes underwater. They have no external ear lobes, but they do hear well.

To prevent manatees from being struck by boats, many areas have speed signage—a no wake zone—indicating that manatees might be

Manatees gather at Crystal River's warm spring during winter. Restrictions apply to boats and divers to protect the large, slow-moving wild animals from human interference.

This West Indian manatee is nursing her calf. Manatee calves stay with their mothers for about two years.

A manatee in a saltwater inlet in the Florida Keys responds playfully to a spray of freshwater. The view is straight down into the large marine mammal's mouth, showing its tongue.

present. However, most manatees I've seen have obvious scarring. I believe most of those scars are the result of being hit by boats. Sometimes those strikes can be lethal. In recent years, 80–97 deaths per year have been recorded, according to the Save the Manatee Club. The manatee population in Florida is only about five thousand animals. They are also subject to threats from nutrient pollution, as mentioned in the chapter on dolphins. Waterfront development has caused the loss of much of the manatee's habitat.

### West Indian Manatee, *Trichechus manatus*

Habitat: coastal waters and rivers. In winter they seek the warmer water of artesian springs and industrial discharge sites.

Size: average 9–10 feet long; over 1,000 pounds.

Diet: herbivorous—freshwater and marine plant life.

Lifespan: more than 50 years.

# River Otter

Cruising along U.S. highway 301/441 south of Gainesville as it was getting dark, I had to slow way down for a pair of North American river otters crossing the highway. I was glad I was traveling slowly enough to be able to avoid the long-bodied, short-legged, thick-furred creatures.

While they crossed the roadway fairly rapidly, they did not seem to be moving as deftly as I'd seen them maneuver, splash, dive, and flash through the water, usually at breakneck speed. Every time I see them having fun in their liquid environment, I can't help but grin.

North American river otters have thick, oily, waterproof coats that once were highly prized by trappers for the fur trade.

Otter pups, weaned by three months of age, stay with their moms for their first year.

River otter pups have to be taught that water is the source of their food. Initially, the youngsters don't want to get wet and are reluctant to learn to swim.

River otter toes are webbed to aid swimming. These otters can stay under water up to eight minutes at a time.

It's hard to take them seriously. They bring joy to my life through the zeal with which they live their lives.

North American river otters have prominent whiskers to help them locate prey underwater. Like manatees, they can close their nostrils and their ears when diving and swimming. An oily coat helps keep them at a comfortable body temperature in the water. Webbed toes assist them in swimming easily, and a thick, heavy tail aids them in changing direction quickly while swimming. They can stay underwater for up to eight minutes.

These otters live in burrows, many of which they borrow from other species, or they choose natural depressions, though they can readily dig for themselves.

A litter of young otters usually numbers two or three. Their eyes don't open until they are about one month old. They're weaned by approximately three months of age, but the pups generally stay with their mother for about a year.

I can often tell otters are nearby when I hear their birdlike chirping sounds. They sound almost as if they're laughing because life is so much fun. River otters are easy to spot when I'm kayaking or canoeing on a waterway, such as the St. Johns River in Florida. Their playful presence assures me that I'm in a healthy ecosystem.

### North American River Otter, *Lutra canadensis*

Habitat: freshwater throughout Florida, except the Keys; creeks, streams, rivers, ponds, lakes, swamps, and mangrove forests.

Size: about 3½ feet or a bit more; 11–30 pounds.

Diet: fish, oysters, and crustaceans, including crayfish and crabs, mollusks, aquatic invertebrates; birds, insects, frogs, turtles, rodents, eggs.

Lifespan: 14 years in the wild.

# Part II

# Birds

# Sandhill Crane

While our Sarasota yard is private, we do share it with another family. Day in and day out throughout the year, a breeding pair of sandhill cranes forage our lawn and planting beds for food. Each spring, they bring around their tiny offspring, showing them the way to a marshy freshwater conservation area right behind us. Our cat, which spends much of his time on our screened lanai, is fascinated by these tall gray birds and is perhaps a bit in awe of their size.

The species is named for the Sandhills of Nebraska, where more than half a million of the large birds congregate each year around March on the way north toward their breeding grounds. "Our" birds have never seen the valley of the Platte River in Nebraska; these cranes belong to a subspecies that remains in Florida year-round.

Sandhill cranes are majestic, proud-looking birds with their unique red caps, which are featherless.

We share our yard with a pair of sandhill cranes. Each spring the cranes bring their new family to see us. Chicks stay dependent on their parents longer than in most bird species.

As can often happen when people move into wildlife habitats, this family of cranes is comfortable living near humans. Cranes mate for life, and it seems as if the couple is showing us their beautiful babies for our approval. It makes us feel they're almost part of our family, and we especially look forward to seeing the little ones each spring.

While the adults are gray, with red caps of skin and white cheeks, the chicks are a tawny brown. The red caps do not show up until maturity, when the cranes can reach a height of four feet. As they move through our yard, they peck at the earth and garden, searching for insects and grubs. Sandhills also eat plants and seeds, frogs and reptiles, even small mammals. In and around Nebraska's Sandhills they favor corn left in fields after autumn's harvest.

These majestic, tall birds can be seen in much of Florida but are seldom seen west of Perry in Taylor County and U.S. highway 221. They're somewhat less frequently seen in extreme south Florida but

One sandhill chick is always significantly larger than the other as the two eggs are not laid, nor hatched, on the same day.

are found in the Everglades. Migratory sandhill cranes add to their numbers in our state from October through March.

We enjoy sharing our yard with this avian family. We still marvel when one of these big birds flies overhead. And it's great fun to photograph them, with a fairly long lens, when they're around. For us, they add a lot to the joy of living in Florida.

## Sandhill Crane, *Grus canadensis pratensis*

Habitat: much of the Florida peninsula—prairies, marshes, pastures, golf courses, open grassy areas.

Size: stands about 3–4 feet tall; wingspan of nearly 7 feet.

Diet: insects, grubs, frogs, small reptiles, plants, seeds.

Lifespan: 20 years or more.

A sandhill crane, looking imperial, stands next to a wood stork near the Venice landfill site.

# Crested Caracara

On the eastern edge of Lake Okeechobee, northwest of Indiantown, I was astonished to see a crested caracara taking a bath in the dust. After all, the lake's water was only a few yards away.

Annoying little creatures, such as lice, bother birds and most other wildlife. Bathing helps get rid of some of these pests. It is the mechanics of bathing—the scraping and polishing—that accomplishes relief. And dirt seems to work just as well as water, as bison out West have also shown me.

A long lens helped me record a crested caracara taking a dust bath, but when I moved in a bit closer after the bath was completed, the caracara flew into a nearby tall palm tree where its mate was waiting. The two birds seemed to check each other. Then they flew away with strong, easy strokes of their wings, which span about four feet. The wings are rounded and show large white patches near the tips. The caracara also has white at the base of its tail.

Almost as big as the more commonly seen black vulture and osprey, the crested caracara is found in central and southern Florida, though sightings have been recorded in the Panhandle. It is a bird of prey, a raptor in the falcon family, but crested caracaras are also scavengers with a highly varied diet. They successfully compete with vultures over carrion.

The caracara is comfortable on the ground, as my photographs show. Its long legs give it good speed when afoot. It's the national bird of Mexico. The Florida subspecies is known as Audubon's crested caracara.

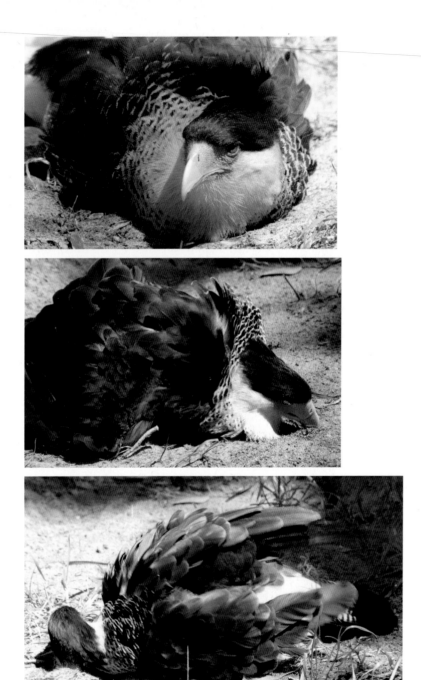

A crested caracara takes a bath in dust very close to Lake Okeechobee.

The end result of the bath is a handsome, distinguished, strong-looking bird.

## Crested Caracara, *Caracara plancus audubonii*

Habitat: central and southern Florida—savannas, palm groves, prairie.

Size: body just under 2 feet long; wingspan about 4 feet.

Diet: most varied of the raptors—small animals and carrion.

Lifespan: about 25 years.

# Vultures

As I drive around Florida, I look up and see large birds soaring over-head or perched in trees (often dead trees) almost everywhere I go. They are dark birds, and they flap their wings very little as they take advantage of thermal updrafts to circle endlessly.

Two species of vultures, or buzzards, are found throughout the state—black and turkey vultures. Black vultures hold their wings al-most straight out as they soar. Turkey vultures' wings are held in a soft V-shape for soaring. Both species are here year-round.

Although considered not very good looking by most people, these birds toil at the important task of cleaning up their domain, eating

Black vultures rely on their vision to find carrion, or they simply let turkey vultures lead them to food.

A black vulture lands next to a turkey vulture (*left*) and another black vulture in Myakka River State Park.

the carrion and garbage that could lead to the spread of disease to humans if left on the ground.

Turkey vultures are the larger of the two species. Their red heads make them easy to identify while immature turkey vultures have gray heads. Neither species has feathers on the head, which helps them avoid carrying unwanted food matter that might lead to sickness for them.

The black vulture is the more aggressive species and often pushes turkey vultures away from food that the turkey vultures may have spotted first. Black vultures are often led to a meal by the dark brown turkey vultures whose excellent sense of smell helps them find food. Without the aid of turkey vultures, black vultures must rely on their sight to find a meal.

I like to watch these hard-working birds soar. Though gangly on the ground, they are graceful in the air as they search for food. I'm pleased to have them continually on duty as a diligent cleanup squad.

A scene often observed in Florida: black vultures on a dead tree.

Black vultures in Ellie Schiller Homosassa Springs Wildlife State Park. These individuals are actually wild, not captive. Note the light wing tips, which are conspicuous when the birds are in flight.

## Black Vulture, *Coragyps atratus*

Habitat: throughout Florida, including the Everglades; mainly open landscapes and lightly wooded areas.

Size: body about 2 feet long or a little less; wingspan of about 4½ feet.

Diet: carrion and garbage; will also take live young birds and mammals.

Lifespan: an average of 10 years; can reach 25 years.

● ● ●

## Turkey Vulture, *Cathartes aura*

Habitat: throughout the state, including the Everglades; mainly forested and woody areas and farmlands.

Size: body length 2–2½ feet; wingspan of 6 feet.

Diet: carrion and garbage.

Lifespan: up to 16 years in the wild.

# Wood Stork

The only stork to be found in the United States is the wood stork. It has been listed as an endangered species since 2013. This stork's dark head and neck are without feathers. Wood storks are long-legged waders that live throughout Florida, principally in cypress swamps and mangroves.

I counted seventeen of these endangered wood storks one day in a

A group of wood storks gathers near the Venice landfill.

A dispute between two wood storks.

small pond within a couple of blocks of my home. And they weren't the only birds in or around that pond.

I watched the storks slowly work their way from one end of the pond to the other, moving their long downward-curved beaks back and forth through the water. They shuffled their feet to stir up fish or other creatures. I also saw their successes. They captured both fish and lizards (or very small gators), sometimes fighting over the catch.

These endangered birds have now lost the little pond that seemed to serve them so well. A new development has recently eradicated

A wood stork searches the water for food.

that small body of water. It's totally dry there now, though there are no homes actually situated where the pond used to be. Loss of habitat like that unfortunately reduces the number of wood storks to be found in Florida today.

### Wood Stork, *Mycteria americana*

Habitat: throughout Florida, including the Everglades, especially coastal mangroves and cypress swamps.

Size: body length about 3½ feet; wingspan up to 5 feet.

Diet: fish and other aquatic animals including amphibians and snails; lizards and insects.

Lifespan: 11–18 years.

A wood stork flies over a Manatee County pond.

# Herons

There are four different species of herons in Florida that are blue or blue-gray in color: the great blue, the little blue, the tricolored heron, and the yellow-crowned night-heron. I've found all four of these wading birds to be most interesting to observe.

I have photographed them all around the state, including in the Everglades, Lido Key, Merritt Island National Wildlife Refuge, and Ding Darling National Wildlife Refuge.

One unfortunate great blue, which had what looked like a painful crippled leg, helped itself by begging for food from people picnicking on Lido Key. It was a beautiful bird, but it saddened me to see its plight.

On the other hand, not far from that picnic spot with its begging great blue, I had the opportunity to watch another great blue heron catching a fish from the Gulf of Mexico's waters for its dinner. At first, the fish was captured crosswise in the bird's heavy bill. With a little adjustment, by tossing the fish slightly and quickly grabbing it again, the great blue maneuvered the fish so that the bird was able to swallow it lengthwise—an exhibition of total control by the great blue heron.

Sometimes, though, the herons look to people for a touch of help. I've seen the big birds station themselves close to people who are surf-fishing, apparently hoping to pick up some leavings. When fishermen catch a fish, they often clean it right on the beach. The discarded parts make a good meal for herons not too shy to be close to people.

A chick seems to mimic its great blue heron parent on their nest in a Venice rookery.

The tricolored heron is about two-thirds the size of the great blue. It has rust-colored or reddish brown feathers on the neck and white underparts (chest and belly). The tricolored is the species of heron most often seen in Florida.

I followed a tricolor along the edges of a canal in the Everglades, photographing it. The bird walked purposefully, constantly scanning the edges of the canal. Frogs and aquatic insects are favorites for this species. In the water, an alligator followed the medium-sized heron. It did not seem to bother the bird to be stalked like that, but it was probably a good thing that the heron did not stand in the water and wait for a fish to come by, as this species often does. Though it didn't appear to be harassed, the heron did eventually fly away easily to continue hunting for food elsewhere.

The little blue heron is about the same size as the tricolor. However, there are no white feathers on the little blue, and it has a reddish brown or maroon neck. This blue-gray bird's diet is mainly insects and grubs. In Ding Darling National Wildlife Refuge, I watched a little blue heron wade offshore in a lagoon in water up to its belly. In

This little blue heron is stalking prey.

Everglades National Park is home to these tricolored herons.

that particular habitat, the heron looked as if it was swimming, but the bird was actually walking slowly through the water looking for prey.

On Sarasota's Lido Key beach, I watched a yellow-crowned night-heron walk from the water's edge into an area that had been protectively cordoned off so that beachgoers would not disturb nesting birds. Though called night-herons because they hunt actively after dark, these slightly smaller herons can also be seen in daylight, as my photographic experience reveals. They favor crabs and crayfish, and their short but powerful beaks can readily crush the exoskeletons of these crustaceans.

Two other heron species are to be found in Florida—the black-crowned night-heron (a black, gray, and white bird) and the green heron. The green is the smallest of the herons, and it is frequently seen.

A green heron prepares to grab a meal in Everglades National Park.

A yellow-crowned night-heron walks by quickly on Lido Key beach. Its crown changes from white to somewhat yellow during breeding season.

Stalking prey in the Everglades, this green heron looks absolutely determined to find something to eat.

A great blue heron on Lido Key in Sarasota.

There is also a white morph or color phase of the great blue heron, found only in south Florida. This large white bird with yellow-green legs has been named the great white heron (though it is not a separate species) and is larger than the similar-looking great egret, which has black legs.

I enjoy seeing blue skies and blue birds. Florida gives me lots of opportunities to enjoy the color blue, one of my favorite colors.

# Egrets

Just before sunup one morning I set up my tripod, mounted my camera on it, and waited for daylight to fully reveal the island in front of me. I was in Venice. The island is a small one, surrounded by water, which I'd been told was patrolled by an alligator.

For the birds nesting in great numbers on that small island, the alligator provided protection from animals that prey on bird eggs and little nestlings. The nesting birds knew a good thing when they found it. And photographers know a good thing when they see it.

Photographing birds on their nests that day was easy. The band of water separating the island from the land where I stood was quite narrow. There were anhingas, great blue herons, and egrets in various stages of parenthood, but it was a pair of snowy egrets that captured much of my attention.

Snowy egrets are medium-sized white birds, and this pair was still busily building their nest. The male would fly in with a stick in his bill, land in a tree close to his mate, and pass the stick from his beak to hers. She would then turn and place the stick in the expanding nest exactly where she wanted it, making little adjustments to get it arranged just so, then wait for him to come in with another stick. She might reposition each stick several times before she was satisfied with its placement. Captivating to watch!

Once the eggs are laid, incubation takes about three weeks. Some of the pair's neighbors already had chicks hatched in their nests. Others were sitting on eggs, waiting. The neighborhood was very busy with all the comings and goings of birds caring for their young. Some of those with chicks were grooming themselves; others were fussing

A male snowy egret brings in a stick and passes it to the female, which turns to add it to the nest they're building. During breeding season they grow delicate plumes on their heads, necks, and backs.

Snowy egrets are readily identified by their slender black bill and yellow feet. Young snowies also have a yellow stripe up the backs of their legs.

over their little ones, while still others were flying back and forth, foraging and carrying food back to the nestlings. It was all right there in front of me—a virtual photographer's paradise.

Florida is home to three species of white egrets. The largest of the three is the great egret. It has gone through several other names, but now "great egret" has been adopted. Snowy egrets are midsized. Cattle egrets are the smallest of these three. Cattle egrets did not arrive in Florida until the 1940s. They came from Africa to South America, then traveled northward and settled here.

Great egrets have yellow bills and black legs and feet.

As cattle move through a pasture they stir up insects and grubs, providing food for cattle egrets. The egrets help keep down the population of flies, thus providing the cattle some relief from those pests.

There also is a reddish egret, which, as its name suggests, is not always white, though there is a white phase. However, it is not so much reddish, as the name indicates, but rather slate-colored, with some reddishness to its head and neck.

The snowy and great egrets were hunted for their spectacular long, showy breeding plumage used often in women's fashions during the late 1800s and early 1900s—hunted almost to extinction. Fortunately, protests arose and human demand for feathers to wear waned, and the two species recovered and are still here in Florida for us to admire.

### Snowy Egret, *Egretta thula*

Habitat: throughout Florida, including the Everglades—ponds, swamps, marshes, and mudflats.

Size: body length nearly 2 feet; wingspan 3½ feet.

Diet: small fish and aquatic insects.

Lifespan: 12–17 years.

• • •

A great egret seems a bit out of place in a tree.

### Great Egret, *Casmerodius albus*

Habitat: throughout Florida, including the Everglades—both saltwater and fresh marshes, ponds, and tidal flats.

Size: stands over 3–3½ feet tall; wingspan 4½ feet.

Diet: fish, frogs, crayfish, and aquatic insects.

Lifespan: about 15 years.

• • •

### Cattle Egret, *Bubulcus ibis*

Habitat: most of Florida, northernmost parts of the state in summer only; prefers open fields, pastures, but breeds near water.

Size: body length less than 2 feet; wingspan about 3 feet.

Diet: insects, grubs, and small mammals.

Lifespan: 6–8 years on average.

• • •

## Reddish Egret, *Egretta rufescens*

Habitat: southernmost Florida, including the Everglades—salt and brackish water in shallow bays, lagoons, and mangrove swamps.

Size: body length about 2½ feet; wingspan nearly 4 feet.

Diet: fish, frogs, and crustaceans.

Lifespan: over 12 years.

The reddish egret is slate-colored with a shaggy reddish head and neck. It is usually seen in shallow bays and lagoons, like this one on Sanibel Island.

# Anhinga

These birds are almost everywhere in Florida, and they easily stand out. With wings spread, almost as if they were worshiping the bright, warming sun, anhingas (and cormorants), unlike other water bird species, have to dry their feathers in this unique manner because they lack the oil glands necessary to repel water.

The lack of oil glands might also be the reason they swim with their bodies submerged in the water. Only the head and long neck are visible when an anhinga is swimming this way. That has led to

This scene of a male anhinga with its wings spread to dry out in the sun is repeated all over Florida.

An anhinga male with its chicks in their nest in Everglades National Park.

The female anhinga has a brown head and neck.

Anhinga chicks, which hatch naked, grow soft, white down before they turn dark like the adults. The chicks are fed regurgitated fish by the parents.

anhingas also being called snakebirds. Having water-soaked feathers probably assists them in making their dives in pursuit of fish. They're very agile underwater.

While this lack of oil glands might seem inconvenient, the anhinga has adapted to be very efficient at catching fish. It has a long, sharp beak with sawlike notches along the edges, creating the perfect implement for spearing a meal. Once the meal is impaled, a quick toss into the air allows the bird to catch the fish at a suitable angle and swallow it headfirst.

I've often seen anhingas soaring in circles, somewhat in the manner of vultures and birds of prey, but the anhinga can be identified by its long neck and fan-shaped tail.

## Anhinga, *Anhinga anhinga*

Habitat: throughout Florida, including the Everglades—freshwater, heavily vegetated swamps and ponds; requires tall trees for nesting.

Size: body length about 3 feet; wingspan nearly 3½ feet.

Diet: fish, crustaceans, and aquatic insects.

Lifespan: 14–16 years.

While anhingas and cormorants are similar in appearance, this Everglades-dwelling double-crested cormorant (*Phalacrocorax auritus*) clearly shows the curve in the end of its beak that is unique to this species.

# White Ibis

South Florida has the greatest population of white ibis, but they can be found throughout Florida. Their down-curving pinkish bills and legs and all-white bodies make them rather easy to identify. They're even easier to identify during breeding season when the bill and legs turn bright red.

White ibis stand nearly two feet tall, with a wingspan of about three feet. Their wings are tipped in black, which is visible only in flight.

The long bill of a white ibis is used to penetrate the subsoil in

A white ibis searches for crayfish or crabs. The red downward-curved bill and red legs are key features in their identification.

Two white ibis and a glossy ibis (*Plegadis falcinellus*). They can often be found together on coastal freshwater ponds and marshes, as shown here in Manatee County.

search of food, which includes crustaceans of all kinds, aquatic insects, and fish. It's fun to watch a group of ibis moving along the water's edge like a well-rehearsed chorus line, poking into the sand, making a find, eating, then moving a few paces to probe again—all in a dance together. They're busy but graceful, poetic creatures, as I discovered on my first trip to Sanibel Island.

The success of white ibis finding food contributes to an increase in the populations of both fish and plankton. White ibis reduce the population of crustaceans that eat fish eggs, and the ibis fertilize the water with their droppings, which provides nutrients for plankton, a basic food source and a critical link in the aquatic food chain. The population of these intriguing birds is holding steady.

Recently I saw a flock of nearly fifty white ibis searching successfully for food on a wide, grassy median in a road near my home in Manatee County. They were working down the length of that median in diagonal lines that stretched from one curb to another. They seem able to find meaningful quantities of food in many different kinds of terrain, even at some distance from shorelines.

White ibis often gather in flocks of thirty or more birds. This small flock of a dozen is in Venice.

Though white ibis prefer freshwater, they will search for food along the Gulf of Mexico's shores, like this group on Sanibel Island.

The reliance of the aquatic ecosystem on white ibis is especially visible near a large colony of these birds. Nature's cycle of life is interdependent and functions well. White ibis fill their role admirably.

## White Ibis, *Eudocimus albus*

Habitat: throughout Florida, including the Everglades—marshes, lagoons, mudflats, swamplands; prefers freshwater, but not exclusively.

Size: body length about 2 feet; wingspan just under 3 feet.

Diet: crustaceans, including crayfish and crabs; aquatic insects; fish.

Lifespan: up to 16 years in the wild.

# Purple Gallinule

I could hardly believe my eyes the first time a highly colorful purple gallinule flew onto the large Everglades lily pads floating on the water in front of me. First, the color of the bird—its gaudy red, blue, green, purple, and yellow adornments—dazzled my eyes.

The purple gallinule looks as if it's walking on water, but it's actually walking on floating leaves. Widespread long toes distribute the gallinule's weight over a relatively large area, providing the colorful Everglades dweller this unique ability.

But then it began to walk from lily pad to lily pad in its hunt for something tasty to eat, like a snail or insect. Its oversized feet and widespread long toes distribute its weight so much that, though the bird was not actually walking on water, it looked almost as if it was!

In addition to the purple gallinule's ability to walk on floating leaves, it will also clamber up onto low-hanging bushes to seek food. It is a swimmer but not a very strong flier.

The riotous rainbow of bright colors and the bird's unique ability to skip along on floating vegetation brought delight to my senses that day in the Everglades.

### Purple Gallinule, *Porphyrula martinica*

Habitat: southern peninsular Florida, including the Everglades, year-round; northern Florida principally in summer; mainly freshwater marshes (with lily pads and/or pickerelweed or other vegetation), ponds and swamps.

Size: body length nearly 1 foot; wingspan less than 2 feet.

Diet: snails and other mollusks, insects, frogs, berries, and seeds.

Lifespan: up to 22 years.

# Beach Birds

Florida is surrounded by beaches, and those beaches are visited by many different species of birds. Florida provides waterways, beaches, marshes, and islands that serve as habitat for many species of shore and wading birds. And the state is also part of a major migratory bird flyway. I find it very pleasurable to watch all these birds, both resident species and migratory ones.

Our routine is to set up our beach towels and folding chairs to enjoy another day at the beach. My wife begins to walk the water's edge, head down, looking for unique shells (she has found all the ordinary shells she wants after years of doing this). I settle into my beach chair,

A snowy plover adult (*left*) and chick share a Sarasota beach.

The laughing gull is one of the most frequently seen birds on Sarasota beaches. Florida Panhandle beaches have a contingent of laughing gulls too.

A laughing gull "laughing." The black cap is only seen during breeding season. In winter they lose their hoods.

turn on my camera, remove the lens cap, and wait, anticipating the birds that may wander by our position on the beach. I'm never disappointed. I've found that I capture better photographs by waiting for birds to come to me rather than by moving out and searching for them.

Perhaps the species I see most often on the beach is the laughing gull. This bird has earned its name because the sound it makes is much like someone laughing. It is most notable for its agility in the air. It swoops, hovers, dives, and calls out loudly to retrieve bits of food that beachgoers may toss into the air. Unfortunately, the population of this aerial acrobat is diminishing, in part due to aggression from herring gulls preying on both the eggs and young of the laughing gull.

Another frequent passer-by is the ring-billed gull. It's larger than the laughing gull, but not as large as the herring gull, though its col-

Ring-billed gulls are also numerous on Florida beaches, especially in winter.

oring is quite similar to the latter's. The black ring around its bill constitutes its most distinctive marking.

I chuckle every time I see a royal tern. To me it resembles a bald man with a wispy monk's fringe of hair. The fringe sticks out from its head more when it is making a statement or courting. This tern is a fish eater. The common tern and other fish-eating terns are noted for their dramatic plunge dives into the water to capture fish. Several other species of tern seem to favor crustaceans and other marine invertebrates. Terns breed in large colonies.

Snowy plovers are difficult to see because of their small size, pale coloring, and swift movement, but watching them scurry across the sand flats is a delight. I encountered a couple of pairs in an area on the beach that had been cordoned off to protect their nests from curious humans. My very long lens allowed me to see them up close and to capture photographs of them. The chicks stayed hidden much of the time, but they did venture into view when the adults raced across

A snowy plover wears its summer attire.

Royal terns enjoy a Venice beach.

This is the winter plumage on a royal tern.

my field of vision. Usually, the adult birds, tiny as they are, stayed between me and their chicks to protect their young.

Many other shorebirds and water birds—sandpipers, plovers, sand-erlings, stilts, oystercatchers, other terns, gulls, larger ibis, herons, and more—will wander by you on Florida beaches. They're searching, each species in its own unique way, for food in the shallow water or along the sandy shorelines that have helped make Florida enticing to so many people. Still other birds, like swift-flying skimmers and squadrons of brown pelicans, will pass before you on the wing. As they parade by, sit back and watch the amazing variety show.

Brown pelicans run across the water's surface to get lift during takeoffs.

The only pelican in the world that is not white is the brown pelican (*Pelecanus accidentalis*), seen here cruising close to the water's surface just off the beach near the North Jetty in Venice. Brown pelicans plunge into the surf with wings half folded. Adults have white heads.

The larger American white pelican (*Pelecanus erythrorhynchos*) can also be seen in Florida. These birds prefer marshy lake and coastal lagoon habitats. During breeding season, they grow strange-looking "horny plates" on their upper bills, which fall off after eggs have been laid.

The herring gull—a juvenile stands at the water's edge—is larger than a laughing gull (*left*) or the ring-billed gulls (*right*).

A juvenile herring gull waits in shallow water to see what the waves might bring.

## Herring Gull, *Larus argentatus*

Habitat: Florida's coastal beaches, mainly in winter.

Size: large, full-chested gull; body length about 2 feet; wingspan 4½ feet or more. Adults are gray and white with pink legs; yellow bill has red spot on lower mandible.

Diet: scavenges mainly for aquatic and marine animals as well as for berries; will drop clams on rocks to break them open.

Lifespan: up to 32 years.

• • •

## Laughing Gull, *Larus atricilla*

Habitat: coastal Florida (rarely inland)—estuaries, bays, and salt marshes.

Size: body length about 16 inches; wingspan 3½ feet or more.

Diet: fish and aquatic invertebrates, squid, crabs, bird eggs and chicks, carrion.

Lifespan: up to 20 years.

• • •

## Ring-Billed Gull, *Larus delawarensis*

Habitat: throughout Florida—saltwater coastal areas, especially in winter, plus freshwater lakes, ponds, streams, and rivers; nests in large colonies.

Size: body length 18–20 inches; wingspan about 4 feet.

Diet: scavenges for fish, invertebrates, and a wide variety of food refuse.

Lifespan: most live 3–10 years, but spans of 23 years have been recorded.

• • •

## Royal Tern, *Sterna maxima*

Habitat: spotty on Florida beaches, except in winter when its presence expands.

Size: body length 18–21 inches; wingspan approximately 3½–4½ feet.

Diet: principally small fish, some aquatic invertebrates.

Lifespan: about 17 years.

• • •

### Snowy Plover, *Charadrius alexandrinus*

Habitat: southwest and northeast Florida—flat, sandy beaches and other large, flat sandy or salt areas.

Size: body length approximately 6 inches; wingspan about 1 foot.

Diet: invertebrates, small crustaceans, mollusks, marine worms, aquatic insects, and seeds.

Lifespan: approximately 11 years.

• • •

### Brown Pelican, *Pelecanus occidentalis*

Habitat: saltwater coastal areas year-round, including shallow estuaries and offshore sand bars; breeds on mangrove islands.

Size: body length approximately 4–4½ feet; wingspan about 7–8 feet.

Diet: small fish in schools near the surface of the water, including mullet, anchovies, and herring; invertebrates such as prawn; scavenges dead animals; will steal fish from other birds.

Lifespan: 10–25 years or more.

• • •

### White Pelican, *Pelecanus erythrorhynchos*

Habitat: in winter only, coastal lagoons and estuaries, especially on the Gulf coast.

Size: body length approximately 5–6 feet; wingspan about 9 feet.

Diet: mainly fish including shiners and jackfish; will steal fish from other birds.

Lifespan: up to 25 years.

# Roseate Spoonbill

Sometimes mistaken for the more familiar pink flamingo, the roseate spoonbill is also a tall and primarily pink bird, but this one comes with one of the most unusual bills to be seen on any bird. It is spoon shaped.

This unique shape serves a specific purpose. Interestingly, though, newly hatched babies do not have the species-specific, spoon-shaped bill. Instead, it begins to widen when the roseate is about fourteen to sixteen days of age. Until then, there is no spoon on a little spoonbill.

The roseate spoonbill's unique bill is shaped for filtering out food as the big bird wades through the water slowly sweeping its slightly opened bill from side to side.

At a small, shallow pond in Manatee County close to my home, I hunkered down in a makeshift blind before sunrise to photograph whatever birds happened to walk in front of me. There were wood storks, great egrets, great blue herons, and an immature bald eagle that flew into one of the bordering trees, as did a kingfisher.

A couple of roseate spoonbills captured my full attention. The tall, red-eyed birds waded slowly through the water, swinging their partially submerged and partly opened bills back and forth through the water. When that bill touched something edible, it snapped shut. Then the bird swallowed the tidbit and continued its filtering search. Yes, the spoon-shaped bill acts as a spoon (by definition, a utensil for eating or stirring).

A roseate spoonbill in Merritt Island National Wildlife Refuge. It's obvious how this tall beauty got its name.

Roseate spoonbills
settle down to roost
for the night on a
small island.

Adult roseate spoonbills are bald and feature red markings and an orange-red tail, in addition to the rosy pink prominent on their wings and bodies. The species was hunted extensively during the late nineteenth and early twentieth centuries for its primary feathers, which were used in ladies' fans or as plumes in their hats. Happily, the hunting has long since ceased and the population has increased. Spoonbill populations in Florida's northern counties and along the shores of the Gulf of Mexico are stable the Audubon Society reports.

However, spoonbill populations in southern Florida, including the area from the Everglades through the Keys, are in decline. This could be due to poor water management of the Everglades, where salinity and water depth are no longer optimal for these specialized wading birds.

Nesting and breeding take place in the dry season for roseate spoonbills. When water levels in ponds and streams are low, food is more plentiful for the big birds and easier to find.

Nests are large and deep, made of sticks. Each nest begins when a single stick is presented to a female by a courting male. The nest usually contains two or three eggs. The chicks hatch with pink skin but no feathers. Early downy feathers are white.

These birds nest in colonies, which I've been lucky enough to see around Florida, principally in the southern part of the state.

Some people regard roseate spoonbills as indicators of the overall health of the Everglades ecosystem. These colorful birds eat fish, and the fish require healthy aquatic vegetation, which in turn requires sufficient inputs of freshwater. For maximum biodiversity this whole circle of life is essential.

### Roseate Spoonbill, *Ajaia ajaja*

Habitat: coastal Florida, including the Everglades, year-round; central peninsular Florida in winter; marshes, swamps, ponds, and rivers; both fresh- and saltwater wetlands.

Size: stands more than 2½ feet tall; wingspan up to 4½ feet.

Diet: small fish, aquatic invertebrates, crustaceans, snails, leeches, worms, amphibians, and some plants.

Lifespan: average 10–16 years; one has been recorded to 28 years.

# Owls

Florida is home to five species of the "wise owls" of legend. I've been able to photograph all five of them during my travels around the state: barn, barred, burrowing, eastern screech, and great horned owls. The latter species is the most widely distributed owl in the United States and one I got to meet up close and personal.

Our backyard had a row of evergreen trees across the back perimeter. They were Christmas trees we'd planted, one each year. When they had reached maturity, tall and beautiful, a great horned owl took up residence in one of them.

My wife was the first to spot the big bird perching serenely in one of those trees. Binoculars helped us see that the owl's eyes were closed—she was sleeping. We continued to see her there day after day.

Ear tufts lying flat, this great horned owl doesn't show the feathers that earned it its name.

We also detected a lot of activity, but the nest she and her mate were remodeling and refurbishing was not visible from our yard. In time, the telltale signs of an owl up above were visible. Owls have a unique adaptation. While they may sometimes swallow prey whole, they can regurgitate those parts that are not digestible, like teeth, bones, and fur. These signs gather as pellets on the ground below. The pellets are a signal that an owl lives here. We found pellets accumulating under that tree. By carefully examining the pellets, smaller than my thumb in size, I could identify some of the prey, including skunks.

Unfortunately, our owls fledged their young when we were away, and we did not get photographs of those chicks carefully moving over time from the well-concealed nest to flight.

Great horned owls generally do not build nests. I know there was a crow's nest in that tree previously. Perhaps that nest was expanded to accommodate our backyard owls.

All owls are raptors, or birds of prey. In all the Florida species except

The great horned owl is the most widely distributed owl in the United States. This big owl has been known to attack humans who ventured too close to its nest.

With its eyes zeroing in on its prey, a great horned owl drops down silently for a meal.

the burrowing owl, the female is the larger bird. As is well known, owls tend to be nighttime hunters (nocturnal). Again, the burrowing owl is an exception; it's active in the daytime (diurnal). Two key components of an owl's superb hunting capability are its acute hearing and its ability to see in very low light. The birds do not have external ears, though some, like the great horned owl, have feathers on the head that give the appearance of ears. Owls fly almost silently because they have barbed feathers, which make little noise as the air passes through them. Burrowing owls tend to sit and wait for prey to get close enough for easy capture.

All owl species are beneficial to humans since they help control the populations of mice, rats, and squirrels, which people often consider pests. Owls therefore provide a sort of biological pest control. In fact, owls are sometimes encouraged by farmers, through provision of nest boxes and perches, to help control those rodent species that destroy crops. Unfortunately, owls and other raptors are often accidentally poisoned by second-generation anticoagulants after consuming

You are more likely to hear a barred owl, like this one in Corkscrew Swamp Sanctuary, than to see one.

The barred owl flies away quickly when anything or anyone makes it nervous.

It's common to see burrowing owls standing on the ground, but normally they're not "dancing" like this (*left*). Bright yellow eyes and distinct white eyebrows distinguish the burrowing owl (*right*).

poisoned rodents. We need to use only safe, cost-effective alternatives now available.

The U.S. Environmental Protection Agency, in a July 2004 report, indicated that the anticoagulant warfarin caused a low to medium secondary effect on birds and mammals. The report also stated that the non-coagulant zinc phosphide had low secondary effects on both birds and mammals. The University of Florida Extension Web site includes trade names for these and other pesticides that are approved for use in Florida. Of course, it is essential to follow label directions when using any of these products, but it is well worth making an effort to minimize the incidence of illness or death in secondary species, such as owls and scavengers.

Here is a quick look at some of Florida's owls, from smallest to largest.

While eastern screech owls are basically nocturnal, they are frequently crepuscular as well; that is, they are active near dawn and dusk. As the photo at right shows, the eastern screech owl wears excellent camouflage that blends in well with its surroundings. Brown, red (or rufous), and gray coloration are equally common in Florida's eastern screech owls.

### Burrowing Owl, *Speotyto cunicularia*

Habitat: plains and fields in southern and central peninsular Florida.

Size: body length about 7½–9¾ inches; wingspan 21½–24 inches.

Diet: tiny mammals, such as moles and mice; insects, including grasshoppers, beetles, and termites; birds, amphibians, reptiles.

Lifespan: about 9 years in the wild.

• • •

### Eastern Screech Owl, *Otus asio*

Habitat: hardwoods, pinelands, swamps, and throughout urban and suburban Florida.

Size: body length 6–9½ inches; wingspan averages 21 inches.

Diet: small prey—songbirds, insects, and rodents.

Lifespan: up to 14 years in the wild.

• • •

Barn owls do not nest only in barns. They also choose dark places in tree cavities and abandoned buildings for their nests.

It's easy to see why almost every description of the barn owl begins with a reference to its heart-shaped face.

## Barn Owl, *Tyto alba*

Habitat: throughout Florida on edges of woods, clearings, farms, and suburbs.

Size: body length 12–15½ inches; wingspan 43–47 inches.

Diet: rodents and insects.

Lifespan: on average about 2 years.

• • •

## Barred Owl, *Strix varia*

Habitat: throughout peninsular Florida including the Everglades; treed swamps and marshes; pine scrubs, forests, prairies, and farms, often near water.

Size: body length 17–19½ inches; wingspan about 43 inches.

Diet: rodents, some birds, invertebrates, amphibians, and reptiles.

Lifespan: 10 years or slightly more in the wild.

• • •

## Great Horned Owl, *Bubo virginianus*

Habitat: throughout Florida, except the Keys—forests, swamps, prairies, and marshes.

Size: body length 18–24½ inches; wingspan 3¼–4¾ feet.

Diet: rodents, rabbits, skunks, opossums, raccoons, squirrels, and occasionally even cats and dogs; owls, turkeys, and other birds.

Lifespan: 5–15 years.

# Falcons and Hawks

In addition to owls and caracaras, the term *raptor* also applies to falcons, hawks, kites, ospreys, and eagles, all to be seen in Florida. These birds of prey are deadly, but beautiful. They hold a specific and important place in nature.

A red-tailed hawk rules our neighborhood. I see it all the time, whirling in the air and issuing its distinctive high-pitched, hoarse-sounding scream from the sky: *keeey, keeey, keeey*. Sometimes I see the bird perched on the peak of a neighbor's roof—waiting and watching.

The most common soaring hawk is the red-tailed hawk; this is a young bird.

One day as I worked at my desk in my home office, I looked out of my window, responding to some strange noises that sounded as if they were just outside. Slowly and carefully I opened the wooden slats of the plantation shutters and discovered that a hawk had landed on my windowsill. It was looking toward my bird feeder, perhaps expecting to find an easy meal there. Not that day.

I picked up my camera with a 400 mm lens, went out through the front door, and quietly walked around to the side of the house. The hawk was still on the windowsill. I began to photograph the bird, taking a step or two closer to try to fill the frame with its image.

Red-tailed hawks are common throughout America, from Florida to Alaska. They especially favor swampy woods and bogs—lowlands with standing water. They often hunt from a low perch, sitting and watching quietly. Roofs are good for that technique, too.

Though the species gets its name from its brick-colored tail, not all red-tailed hawks have red tail feathers.

An immature red-tailed hawk perches on a house roof—waiting and watching for any action in the meadow below.

The two subspecies of red-shouldered hawks in Florida tend to be paler than other red-shouldered hawk subspecies.

Another day I was out on the water with one of my sons, who is a boating enthusiast. As we slowly motored along the Intracoastal Waterway out of Venice, we passed osprey nest after osprey nest, most showing chicks in various stages of development. Ospreys are comfortable building their nests on man-made platforms, like boat markers and other types of pole-based structures.

Once or twice we got too close for the birds' comfort, and we were hollered at in no uncertain terms by a parent. Oops, sorry. Ospreys are fish hawks, and their nesting habits place them close to their food source, the water. The osprey is the only raptor willing to drop right into the water, talons first, to capture its prey rather than simply snatching prey at the surface.

Ospreys often build their nests on platforms provided by humans, such as this position marker for boaters on the Intracoastal Waterway near Venice. Ospreys are often mistaken for bald eagles, but they are smaller and have white underparts, plus a dark line through the eye.

A young osprey exercises its wings to strengthen them before trying flight. Ospreys can hover before dropping down into the water to capture a fish.

The osprey also carries its prey in a unique position—head first, parallel with the bird's body—thereby achieving less wind resistance in flight. The osprey's feet are specially adapted for their slippery prey. Ospreys have particularly long talons, and they have sharp spines on the undersides of their toes for superior grasping ability.

Birds classified as hawks have hooked bills (for tearing flesh) and sharp talons. Many have short, broad tails and wide, rounded wings for soaring. Others have long, narrow tails and short, rounded wings for maneuverability in twisting flight through branches, as needed for flights through dense forests.

Also called sparrow hawks, American kestrels and other falcons have long tails and pointed wings, making them very swift flyers.

There are so many different raptors in Florida that the Audubon Society has established their Center for Birds of Prey in Maitland. They rehabilitate sick and injured birds with the intent of releasing them back into the wild. Some twenty species of raptors are on view at this Audubon Center, which is open Tuesdays through Sundays. There is an admission fee. Not all the birds they care for are releasable back into the wild, due to various physical reasons. They also have a wetland, a boardwalk, and lakeshore.

The American kestrel is the smallest falcon in the United States.

Look for the American kestrel perching on a dead tree snag, a fence post (like this male), or telephone wires.

Raptors have long fascinated me. I suppose it's their handsome good looks and their lethal capabilities that combine to capture my interest.

## American Kestrel, *Falco sparverius*

Habitat: in winter, throughout Florida, including the Everglades, towns and cities, open country, parks, and farms; in summer, central peninsular Florida and the Panhandle.

Size: body length 9–12 inches; wingspan up to 24 inches—the smallest falcon in the United States. The Florida subspecies (*Falco sparverius paulus*) is smaller.

Diet: house sparrows and other small birds; insects, small rodents, and reptiles it captures on the ground.

Lifespan: average 1 year, but can live up to 11 years.

• • •

Red-shouldered hawks like to hunt from a perch.

## Red-Shouldered Hawk, *Buteo lineatus*

Habitat: throughout Florida, including the Everglades, mature forests, and treed swamps with dead trees for perching.

Size: body length 1½–2 feet; wingspan 3–3½ feet.

Diet: small mammals and birds, reptiles, amphibians, insects, and aquatic crustaceans.

Lifespan: average 2 years.

• • •

## Red-Tailed Hawk, *Buteo jamaicensis*

Habitat: in winter, throughout Florida, including the Everglades, forests, farmlands, and other open areas; not present in extreme south Florida in summer.

Size: body length 18–22 inches; wingspan about 4 feet.

Diet: small rodents, including mice and ground squirrels; rabbits; reptiles.

Lifespan: average 21 years.

• • •

## Osprey, *Pandion haliaetus*

Habitat: seacoasts, rivers, lakes, ponds, and wetlands in the Everglades.

Size: body length up to 2 feet; wingspan 5–6 feet.

Diet: fish.

Lifespan: average 30 years.

# Bald Eagle

Just saying the word *eagle* brings thoughts of majesty and strength, skill and empire to my mind. Humans have had those kinds of thoughts about eagles down through almost the entire history of humankind.

We know the bald eagle was chosen as the symbol of the United States because of its strength, power, and dominance of its domain—the skies—giving it freedom. This raptor is found only on the North American continent, and Florida has a strong population. In my experience, only Alaska and Minnesota seem to have more bald eagles than we have right here.

An adult bald eagle develops the highly recognizable white head at between three and four years of age. The word "bald" refers to white feathers, not to a lack of feathers.

Bald eagles can be found throughout Florida.

I have found a number of eagle nests within a very few miles of my home, and I've seen bald eagles all around our state. The Florida Fish and Wildlife Conservation Commission reported more than 1,300 nesting pairs in the state during the 2008–2009 nesting season. Estimates indicate more than 9,700 nesting pairs of bald eagles in the United States.

My first personal encounter with a bald eagle happened when I was about eleven. While on a family vacation I spotted a big white-headed bird rising off the water carrying a fish. To my surprise, an even larger white-headed bird dove down on the bird I was watching. They maneuvered acrobatically, around, up, down, and around again, spinning and turning. Finally the smaller bird dropped its fish and flew off. The attacking bird grabbed the dropped fish in midair and flew away with it.

I did not know it then, but I had witnessed a rather common occurrence—a bald eagle stealing a fish from an osprey. The original fish-catching bird, the osprey, carried the fish head-forward, parallel to its body. The attacking eagle flew off with the fish carried across its body. Ospreys are about two-thirds the size of bald eagles, which are known to take food from both ospreys and crows. The eagles are opportunistic feeders, and they are dominant.

Golden eagles also appear in Florida from time to time, I've been told, but I have never seen one here personally. Immature bald eagles are sometimes incorrectly identified as golden eagles because they lack the adult's white head and tail feathers.

The highly skilled bald eagle prefers to eat fish. Flying at 30–35 miles per hour, it can also take waterfowl out of the air, rabbits running at full speed on the ground, and other small mammals.

Yes, these muscular and powerful birds of prey have captured the respect—even worship—of humans down through the ages. Alexander the Great had coins minted in 310 B.C. with his face on one side

This immature bald eagle appears to be just about ready to get its white head.

and a standing eagle on the reverse. The pharaohs of Egypt also had eagles on their coins. At one time, Egypt had two pharaohs ruling concurrently. The coins minted at that time had two eagles on them. And it's well known that ancient Rome used the eagle symbol to represent that all-powerful nation.

Many nations besides the United States have adopted the eagle to represent them in the modern era, including Russia, Italy, Austria, Germany, Poland, Spain, Imperial France, and others. Old Germanic and Native American cultures believed the eagle was the messenger of the gods.

We know it is a spectacular bird to watch. From my observation of eagle nests, I believe that bald eagles, which mate for life and use the same massive nest year after year, bring a sprig of something fresh and green to their nests each year to indicate to others that the nest is in use. In the Sunshine State, nests are most often seen in tall pines or oaks near water. Nesting season for bald eagles in Florida is between October 1 and May 15. Some of our eagles do fly north after raising their young, so you are more likely to see eagles in Florida during their nesting season.

Bald eagles, I've noted, also maintain a "larder" of stored food somewhere in those huge nests. Those nests are important, but if human activity comes too close, the nesting pair may simply abandon their nest, sometimes with young in it. Florida statutes suggest that human activity be kept 660 feet from eagle nests as a buffer to prevent the birds from abandoning their nests.

Bald eagle mating includes an elaborate aerial dance. At one point, the pair locks their talons together, one bird upside down. Then their easily seen white heads and tails tumble dizzily through the air until they unclasp and fly again. Bald eagles do not obtain the white head and tail until they're about three or four years old. Juveniles are dark brown with white spots scattered over their bodies. Females are larger than males.

Though bald eagles prefer to eat fish, they do not like to go into water to catch fish. They much prefer taking a fish from the surface, grabbing their prey with those sharp talons, or taking it from an osprey in the air. However, I once watched an eagle take a fish on the

A bald eagle sits beside its nest on Longboat Key. If the bird is three feet long, the nest is nearly six feet across and nine feet high. The largest recorded bald eagle nest measured nine and a half feet wide by twenty feet high and weighed over two tons.

surface that proved to be too big for even that mighty bird to lift. The eagle splashed and hopped and thrashed its wings, but it could not fly. Eventually, it got its fish to shore, where the eagle enjoyed a leisurely meal. It's been estimated bald eagles can lift up to four pounds into the air.

Long a symbol of courage, judicious intelligence, and strength, the bald eagle is a wonderful symbol for our nation. Happily, its population in Florida is stable and being maintained. However, we could do

Bald eagles prefer to eat fish, but they will also eat small mammals, like rabbits, and carrion (dead animals). The latter can be the cause of an eagle's death from lead poisoning when small particles of lead from bullets and buckshot lodge in the remains of hunted animals.

Bald eagles do not like to splash in the water but prefer to snatch fish near the surface, putting only their sharp talons into the water to make the grab.

more. Being at the top of the food chain, bald eagles are susceptible to chemical poisoning. Americans witnessed these dynamics after the widespread use of DDT was nationally banned in 1972. Scientists had found that an accumulation of DDT in the birds' tissue resulted in their eggs being thin-shelled, often breaking during incubation, thus causing the population to plummet. It had been estimated in the 1960s that only five hundred breeding pairs of bald eagles remained in the lower forty-eight states. The ban on the use of DDT and passage of the Endangered Species Act in 1973 resulted in the rebound of the bald eagle population. This is considered the first major success of the environmental protection movement. Gray and red wolves, grizzly bears, sea turtles, manatees, and other species also benefited from this landmark legislation.

A bald eagle lands on a tree branch after being released from the Wildlife Center of Venice rehabilitation facility, where the eagle recovered from a broken wing.

Now, many bald eagles, and other animals that eat carrion, are being killed by lead poisoning from eating the remains of animals shot by hunters and left in fields to be scavenged. This unwittingly lethal practice could be resolved by simply replacing lead projectiles with bullets and buckshot made from non-lead materials. These alternatives are currently available, so legal hunting would not be restricted in order to make this life-saving adjustment. I'm simply suggesting that it is time to make an affordable change in what we're putting into our rifles and shotguns. Death by lead poisoning is a slow, agonizing, and horrible way for any creature to die.

I hope we will all work together to preserve and protect our wildlife in these ways. Help make sure that bald eagles—and all wild animals—are here in Florida for our children and our children's children to see and enjoy, as we enjoy seeing and experiencing them now.

### Bald Eagle, *Haliaeetus leucocephalus*

Habitat: throughout Florida, including the Everglades, and along seacoasts, rivers, lakes, and marshes. Panhandle populations tend to migrate north in summer.

Size: body length 2½–3 feet; wingspan up to 7 feet.

Diet: fish, ducks and other birds, carrion.

Lifespan: average 15–20 years; can live up to 30 years in the wild.

# Part III
# **Reptiles**

# American Alligator

In Big Cypress National Preserve one day, I was photographing an American alligator sunning itself on dry land next to a canal. Cold-blooded animals (*ectothermic*), alligators depend on the sun and their environment to provide warmth, both for themselves and for their incubating eggs in a nest. I moved very slowly as I changed positions to get different photographic angles. Deciding I wanted to get some straight-on shots, I lay down on my stomach to place my long lens on the gator's level. I got the shots I wanted.

When I stood up quickly, the gator threw itself into the water and swam a short distance away. My sudden movement had scared the

This alligator is eager and ready to eat in Ellie Schiller Homosassa Springs Wildlife State Park. Gators are found along many Florida rivers and other bodies of freshwater and, sometimes, in brackish water.

twelve-foot-plus alligator. I know better than to move too quickly around wild animals, but my brain does not always seem to remember this important practice when I'm in wildlife's view.

Strong swimmers, alligators are awkward on land. It has been reported that they can outrun humans for short distances in a straight line, but they cannot turn easily. A person threatened by a gator on land should run in a zig-zag pattern.

Alligators are the largest reptiles in North America. They're widespread in Florida. The species is believed to be 150–230 million years old. They co-existed with dinosaurs. There was a time when their numbers were depressed, but hunting restrictions through laws passed in 1967 and 1973 aided their return to acceptable levels. It's estimated that there are now more than a million alligators in America. They were removed from endangered status in 1987. State and federal protections and preservation of vital habitat helped create this significant victory for conservationists. The alligator is Florida's official state reptile.

On spring nights, alligators often gather in a group for courtship rituals described as alligator dances. Biologists study alligators at night

This view of an American alligator is definitely not one you want to see when you're swimming!

Like these Everglades dwellers, alligators are patient when waiting for prey, and they can blend in well with their surroundings.

A view from the gator's level. Alligators have a short, rounded snout and show only top teeth when the mouth is closed. Crocodiles (not shown) are saltwater dwellers that have a narrow, pointed snout and show upper teeth and the fourth tooth on the lower jaw when the mouth is closed. Both species have very powerful jaws.

because it's easy to see their eyes reflecting a red glow from light shining over the water's surface. In daylight, it is much more difficult to spot them in the water.

Alligators are more aggressive during mating and nesting season. A female generally builds a nest by pulling vegetation together into a mound, which may be up to four feet high and eight feet across. She lays twenty to fifty eggs in a cavity in the mound, covers them, and guards her nest. It takes about sixty-five days for the eggs to hatch. The temperature in the nest determines the sex of the hatchlings: temperatures of 93 degrees Fahrenheit or higher produce males; 86 degrees or cooler, females. And those little gators might stay within their mother's protection up to two years. If you come upon baby alligators, watch carefully for mama!

You can see little alligators hatch during the Hatching Festival at Gatorama in Palmdale during August. For a fee, you can even hold an egg while the seven- to nine-inch gator chirps and hatches. A newly hatched gator stays attached to its egg by an umbilical cord for a short while. Crocodiles are also on display at Gatorama.

Alligators are considered adults when they reach six feet in length. The tail makes up about half of a gator's length. Feeding alligators is illegal and also unwise, because the animals then become dependent upon humans. Those who study gators have learned that slapping the water's surface once or twice will bring to the surface those gators accustomed to being fed. An alligator fed by humans will likely be removed and killed as a nuisance animal long before living out its normal lifespan.

Though the sign may seem unnecessary—especially with an alligator so close to it—swimming is reserved for wildlife at Ellie Schiller Homosassa Springs Wildlife State Park.

Deep Hole in Myakka River State Park is one place where you are likely to see hundreds of alligators. It is a four-mile roundtrip, and only thirty people per day are allowed to hike in. You're likely to see white pelicans and black vultures there as well.

Alligators contribute to the well-being of other species by digging holes or depressions that may continue to hold water during extended periods of little or no rain. Those burrows may also be used as winter shelters.

### American Alligator, *Alligator mississippiensis*

Habitat: throughout Florida, including the Everglades, in freshwater rivers, lakes, ponds, swamps, and brackish marshes.

Size: up to 18 feet (average is 13 feet); can weigh 450 pounds or more.

Diet: fish and mollusks; reptiles, including turtles, lizards, snakes, and small alligators; birds and small mammals; carrion. Smaller prey are swallowed whole.

Lifespan: 35–50 years in the wild.

# Rattlesnakes

One warm and sunny day while I searched for a gopher tortoise's burrow, I encountered a tenant that relies heavily on the gopher tortoise providing it a home—a rattlesnake. The eastern diamondback rattler, in particular, favors such burrows. The diamondback lives throughout Florida.

At times, snakes and gopher tortoises actually share one of the tortoise's burrows. And rattlers use abandoned gopher tortoise burrows extensively. On this day I found a handsome timber rattlesnake in residence.

As I watched the burrow from a short distance away, a rattlesnake slowly emerged. It slithered out, heading almost directly toward me. However, I was more than twenty feet away—well past the fifteen-foot distance a rattlesnake can see reliably.

Rattlesnakes are pit vipers, and Florida has three species. The heat-sensing pit organ is located between the nostril and the eye of this eastern timber rattlesnake.

An eastern diamondback rattlesnake in defensive position. Like other pit vipers, this one relies on its tongue and heat sensing "pits" for sensory information.

The Florida Museum of Natural History notes that there are fifty species of snakes in Florida (plus forty-five subspecies), but only six of them are venomous. Three of those venomous species are rattlesnakes: the eastern diamondback, eastern timber or canebrake, and dusky pigmy rattlesnakes. All rattlesnakes are pit vipers, which means they have heat sensitive organs (pits) located between their nostrils and their eyes. These heat sensors are extremely sensitive, giving pit vipers the ability to home in on prey that are not moving or to find prey in absolute darkness.

None of the rattlesnakes living in Florida is particularly aggressive. They can strike about two-thirds of their body length. Therefore the average three-foot-long rattlesnake has a strike zone of about two feet. I placed a pane of glass between this individual and me for my own safety. But it did not strike.

Rattlesnakes can also be found in backyards, in and around homes, on golf courses, and in other habitats. In especially hot weather, they can become nocturnal. Rattlesnakes are good swimmers too.

As with other wildlife I've encountered, like wolves out West, for instance, snakes tend to move away from humans if they're not cornered and feeling the need to defend themselves. They would rather flee than fight. Florida's rattlesnakes are calm and usually slow to strike, often giving an extensive warning with their rattles and showing repeated feinting with their heads. The rattles are only used when the snakes are attempting to defend themselves. When the snakes are hunting for a meal, their rattles remain silent.

Rattlesnakes give live birth to an average of ten to twelve fully formed young every two or three years. Males mature at four to six years of age; females mature a few years later.

The eastern timber rattlesnake inhabits the Panhandle and other northern portions of Florida. Its New England relatives were the models for the Revolutionary-era flag featuring a coiled snake and the motto: "Don't tread on me." That's a good slogan to remember when you're in their territory. Snakes generally help humans by controlling the size of rodent populations, which makes it a good thing to have snakes in your neighborhood. We can coexist with rattlesnakes, as tortoises have also discovered.

Dusky pygmy rattlesnakes prefer cover like pine needles or grass where they can hide and easily ambush their prey. Both this dusky pygmy and the eastern diamondback pictured in this chapter are captives, part of the ongoing education and rehabilitation work being done by Wildlife Inc., located in Anna Maria and Bradenton.

This eastern diamondback is about to shed its skin, as its opaque eyes clearly indicate.

### Eastern Timber Rattlesnake, *Crotalus horridus*

Habitat: northern Florida—forests and swampy areas.

Size: 3–5 feet; 1–2 pounds.

Diet: rodents and other small mammals, birds, frogs, and other snakes.

Lifespan: 20 to 30 years.

• • •

### Eastern Diamondback Rattlesnake, *Crotalus adamanteus*

Habitat: throughout Florida, including the Keys—pine woods, coastal islands, and palmetto thickets.

Size: 3 to 6 feet (there have been reports of an 8-foot individual); 4 to 10 pounds; most are about 3 feet long, weighing 1 to 2 pounds.

Diet: small mammals (chiefly rodents), small birds (especially ground dwellers), frogs, and garter snakes.

Lifespan: about 15 years in the wild.

• • •

### Dusky Pigmy Rattlesnake, *Sistrurus miliarius barbouri*

Habitat: prairies and marshes throughout Florida, except in the Keys.

Size: thick bodied, 1 to 2 feet long.

Diet: principally frogs and mice.

Lifespan: 20 to 30 years.

# Cottonmouth or Water Moccasin

The Florida Panther National Wildlife Refuge was the scene of one of my encounters with a venomous snake: the cottonmouth, also commonly known as a water moccasin. Like other *ectotherms* (cold-blooded animals), this one was sunning itself on a cool, winter day. The snake's broad, flat head and the white display of its wide-open mouth clearly identified its species to me.

Though the cottonmouth has a rather short, thick body, this one pretty well blocked the entire width of the narrow trail I was walking. I pointed my 400 mm camera lens and started taking pictures. The

A short, heavy-bodied snake, the cottonmouth or water moccasin has a dark gray, black, brown, or dark olive body. Sometimes it will coil and shake its tail in a rattlesnake-like behavior.

A cottonmouth snake's most distinctive characteristic is the white lining of its mouth, which it displays as a warning when defending itself.

name cottonmouth comes from the white lining of the mouth that this snake displays in its defensive stance.

As I changed my position to capture different angles, a young couple came up behind me. They asked what I was photographing.

When I told them, they asked, "How are we going to get by safely?" I said I would step over the snake and distract it to get it to look in a different direction. With the snake looking at me, they could move slowly and carefully across and over its tail end and continue on their way. That was what we did. I got more photographs from a different position; they went safely on down the narrow trail.

Cottonmouths are slow to move, even sluggish. This is true especially when the snake is contentedly sunning itself, probably with a well-filled stomach. Cottonmouths are not aggressive; certainly one of the more sedate snakes I've encountered.

Cottonmouths are water snakes, the only venomous water snake in North America. Generally, they're found within a short distance of a body of water or in it. They can strike at prey in the water as well as on land. They do not have to coil to strike. Like rattlesnakes, cottonmouth snakes also have that facial pit between the nostril and the eye for sensing prey through the body heat prey animals radiate. Cottonmouths are principally night hunters.

Female cottonmouth snakes keep their small, fertilized eggs within their bodies and nourish them. Pit vipers, including the cottonmouth, are viviparous, giving birth to up to fifteen live young seven to fourteen inches long. The youngsters are venomous at birth. Breeding is usually an every-other-year event.

Like several other wildlife species profiled in this book, this is an animal that contributes to our comfort by hunting and consuming other species we humans find undesirable. We just need to avoid contact with these co-inhabitants of our environment.

### Cottonmouth or Water Moccasin, *Agkistrodon piscivorus conanti*

Habitat: throughout Florida near water—streams, rivers, ponds, lakes, swamps, and other wetlands.

Size: approximately 2 to 4 feet long, though 6-footers have been reported.

Diet: fish, frogs, other snakes (including their own kind), lizards, small mammals, small birds, and carrion.

Lifespan: 10 to 20 years.

# Gopher Tortoise

It was a very warm summer day. I was walking through a pine woods habitat looking for scrub-jays and other species to photograph. In fact, it was so warm that I had to sit down for a rest on a large rock at the edge of a wooded copse.

I heard sounds of an animal approaching. It obviously did not care if it was heard, which is not what I expect in the wilds. Then it strolled into a clearing. To my surprise, all that noise was being made by a gopher tortoise, a land dweller about ten inches long, as it moved through the dry undergrowth. This is the only tortoise or land turtle species found in Florida.

I aimed my camera at the tortoise. It paused momentarily, as if to offer me the most flattering angle to photograph. The tortoise then proceeded across the open area toward me. I took more photos as it headed directly at me. A threatened species, the tortoise walked into

A gopher tortoise moves right along in Oscar Scherer State Park.

A gopher tortoise's carapace or top shell may be tan to dark gray in color.

my shadow and settled down there. I was providing it with a shaded area on this hot summer afternoon. What a privilege!

While the gopher tortoise is a candidate for the status of a threatened species, it can be found throughout Florida. Its ability to dig burrows that are used by as many as 360 other species, its willingness to share occupancy of those burrows, and its contribution to the maintenance of its environment through spreading seeds all combine to make it a keystone species. It spends a lot of time in these burrows, which average thirty feet in length (but can reach forty-eight feet), nine or ten feet underground. Its front feet are particularly adapted for digging. The burrows provide these terrestrial turtles safe haven from heat, cold, fire, and predators.

Coming around a curve in a street near my home, I discovered a line of six or seven cars stopped in the lane facing me. I wondered, for a moment or two, why those cars were stopped there, blocking traffic. Then I spotted the gopher tortoise in the middle of that lane. Its dark gray color and yellow plastron (lower shell) clearly identified it as a gopher tortoise.

It raised its head as high as it could to look around. I pulled my car out of traffic's way and went over to pick up the tortoise. I put it down away from the road, facing in the same direction it had been heading to cross the road. The tortoise continued safely on its way, as did the stopped vehicles. I knew not all drivers had the patience to wait for a slow-moving tortoise to cross the road. But happily, these people had waited.

Unfortunately, road mortality is one of the main reasons this species is a candidate for threatened status. The gopher tortoise faces four other major threats:

1. Loss of habitat from human development
2. Humans taking them from the wild, both as pets and for consumption
3. Disease
4. Relocation

As Florida's population has grown, more and more gopher tortoises are having their habitats literally bulldozed and cemented over. Builders are now required by Florida law to relocate gopher tortoises found on land they are developing. But these herbivores (plant eaters) do not necessarily stay where they've been taken. And that can lead to more tortoises being at risk from vehicular traffic as they seek a more satisfactory home.

Its 60-million-year span on earth may come to an end. The gopher tortoise is not an especially prolific species. It is solitary except during mating season (most likely May and June). Tortoise courtship might produce three to twenty-five eggs about the size of ping-pong balls. They take eighty to ninety days to hatch. A long list of predators takes

Gopher tortoise eggs are laid in a nest close to the entrance of the female's burrow.

Helpful to many species, the gopher tortoise digs burrows that become homes for other animals.

about 90 percent of the eggs. Any surviving hatchlings, which have yellow carapaces (top shells), can spend up to a year with their mother.

As with alligators, the temperature of the nest determines the sex of the hatchlings. Above 85 degrees Fahrenheit, the youngsters are female; under 85 degrees, they're male.

They reach maturity at ten to fifteen years, by which time their shells measure about nine inches long. Males have a concave plastron, while the bottom shell of females is flat.

In addition to Oscar Scherer State Park in Osprey, where I provided shade for one gopher tortoise, other places with notable populations of gopher tortoise are Eglin Air Force Base near Valparaiso, Apalachicola National Forest near Tallahassee, and the Okefenokee-Osceola longleaf pine ecosystem near Kissimmee.

## Gopher Tortoise, *Gopherus polyphemus*

Habitat: ideally, four acres of longleaf pine ecosystem in sandy soil.

Size: shell about 8–12 inches long, 6–15 inches high at the shell's peak; weight about 29 pounds.

Diet: grasses and legumes (plants that bear pods), fruits and flowers, especially asters and daisies; gets its water from food; drinks standing water only in times of drought.

Lifespan: 40–75 years or more.

# Turtles

As I travel around Florida looking for wild animals to photograph, I frequently see turtles—singly or in groups—basking on logs or along shores of freshwater lakes and streams. Most common among these sun seekers are Florida red-bellied cooters and coastal plain cooters (the latter are sometimes referred to as Florida cooters or river cooters). Both species are also farm raised and sold as pets.

Cooters are often defined as baskers because of their most frequent behavior. All cooters are turtles. Specifically, cooters are large, aquatic turtles.

The term slider is also applied to these freshwater turtles because

A trio of Florida red-bellied cooters basks in warm sunshine beside a canal in the Everglades.

they slide into water when they're approached. Generally, sliders are olive-brown above (carapace) and yellow below (plastron). They belong to the genus *Pseudemys*.

One unique behavior of the red-bellies, which have high domed shells, is their habit of laying their eight to thirty oval eggs in an alligator's nest. This provides the turtle eggs the protection of an alligator guarding the nest. The alligator eggs hatch in about sixty-five days; the turtle eggs incubate for seventy-three to eighty days, so hatchlings of the two species leave the nest at different times even if the eggs were laid at the same time.

Alligators often attack the red-bellies and other turtles. I frequently see individuals with damaged shells, probably due to unsuccessful alligator attacks. Eggs and hatchling turtles are also preyed upon by a number of larger animals, including raccoons, skunks, crows, herons, rats, and bullfrogs.

There are thirty-seven species and subspecies of turtles in Florida.

Everglades National Park is home to this Florida red-bellied cooter. The slightly elongated and somewhat curved foreclaws indicate that this is a male.

They're found in aquatic habitats throughout the state, in both fresh and brackish water.

Cooters are defined as herbivores (plant eaters) but should perhaps be defined as omnivores. In the wild, they supplement their basic veggies with aquatic invertebrates. In the pet trade, the diet recommended includes worms, fish, and insects as well as plants. The U.S. Geological Survey notes they also eat carrion, specifically dead fish.

A recent study indicates that Florida has one of the highest numbers of reptile species threatened with extinction, according to the Center for Biological Diversity. They report that the International Union for the Conservation of Nature blames habitat loss and overharvesting for the problem worldwide. Freshwater turtles are especially threatened with extinction, they note. More than twelve Florida reptiles are imperiled, the nonprofit Center for Biological Diversity reports.

I would much rather discover basking turtles in the wild, along a slow-flowing river, for instance, than have one at home as a captive pet. Just the sight of them lounging in the sun provides me a feeling of tranquility; a feeling that all is right with the world.

### Florida Red-Bellied Cooter, *Pseudemys nelsoni*

Habitat: lakes, ponds, sloughs, canals, ditches; favors plant-rich environments.

Size: 8–15 inches; females average 12 inches, 8–9 pounds; males average 10 inches, about 4 pounds.

Diet: algae and other aquatic plants, aquatic invertebrates, small vertebrates.

Lifespan: approximately 50 years.

• • •

### Coastal Plain Cooter, *Pseudemys concinna floridana*

Habitat: vegetation-rich lakes, ponds, sloughs, canals, and ditches.

Size: 9 –13 inches (one female reportedly reached 16 inches); 5½–7½ pounds.

Diet: algae and aquatic plants, invertebrates, small vertebrates.

Lifespan: 30 or more years in the wild; 40 or more years in captivity.

# Sea Turtles

Knowing our interest in protecting and preserving all wildlife, our eleven-year-old granddaughter Emily suggested we visit the Turtle Hospital on a recent trip to the Florida Keys. She knew we'd see some sea turtles because she had visited there on an earlier trip with her parents, who regularly vacation on a nearby key.

Since sea turtles, saltwater dwellers, spend virtually their entire lives at sea, it's next to impossible for landlubbers and non-divers like me to see and photograph them, except when they come ashore to lay their eggs. Nesting normally occurs at night; the use of flash photography for sea turtles is discouraged, and rightly so. Light can

Green sea turtles are not green, but their body fat is.

Granddaughter Emily holds a hawksbill sea turtle.

disorient the animals, causing them to cut short their egg laying or abandon a nest without covering up the eggs.

We paid a fee for a guided educational visit to this unique hospital in Marathon. We saw some of the turtles there recovering from a variety of injuries, generally caused directly or indirectly by humans. It truly breaks my heart to see so many animals needlessly maimed and hurt because some people simply do not care about or fail to pay attention to the consequences of their actions.

I'm proud to share that from her previous visit, Emily knew that five of the world's seven species of sea turtles are found in Florida waters. The Turtle Hospital's mission is "rescue, rehabilitation and release." Their literature points out that they are "the only state-certified veterinary hospital in the world for sea turtles."

Mote Marine Laboratory in Sarasota also provides care and rehabilitation for ill and injured sea turtles and other marine species,

This Kemp's ridley sea turtle is at Mote Marine Laboratory in Sarasota for special care.

as do the Miami Seaquarium, Sea World in Orlando, and Gumbo Limbo Nature Center in Boca Raton.

Sea turtles are large reptiles. Though they spend their lives in water, they breathe air and lay eggs on land. However, they remain underwater for hours when they are resting or inactive, the U.S. Fish and Wildlife Service notes. One of the differences between sea turtles and other turtles is that the larger sea dwellers cannot retract the head or flippers into their shells. The loggerhead, which is the species most likely to be seen in Florida waters, is listed as a threatened species. All the other sea turtle species are considered endangered.

It's estimated that sea turtles, all of which are highly migratory, have existed for 100 million years. The green turtle is named for its green body fat, not for the color of its shell. Leatherbacks are larger, dive deeper, can endure colder water, and travel farther than other sea turtle species, according to the Florida Fish and Wildlife Conservation Commission. Instead of shells, leatherbacks have a firm but flexible leathery carapace for protection.

Emily pointed out the hawk-like jaw of the hawksbill, which has jaws adapted for harvesting sponges. The Kemp's ridley is the rarest of all sea turtles and the most endangered.

Sea turtles breed every two to five years. Females only come ashore to lay 100–200 eggs, usually in June or July. The eggs are round like ping-pong balls and take about two months to hatch. However, female sea turtles may create nests, which they dig with their back legs, several times per season. As with other reptiles, the temperature in the nest helps determine the sex of the hatchlings. The dividing point seems to be 85 degrees Fahrenheit. Above that temperature, females emerge from the nest; below 85 degrees, males emerge from the nest. At 85 degrees, the sexes are mixed. Sea turtles become sexually mature at ten to twelve years.

About seventy injured sea turtles arrive at the Turtle Hospital every year, they report. Additionally, around a hundred injured or disoriented hatchlings spend some time at the Turtle Hospital every summer. The hospital states it has released more than a thousand turtles back into the wild.

Life for sea turtles begins in a very hazardous way as the hatchlings crawl out of their sandy nests and head toward the nearby sea.

A loggerhead sea turtle comes up for air.

Volunteers put up markers, like this one on a Sarasota beach, to protect sea turtle nests from humans.

Only about one in a thousand survives to maturity. All along Florida's extended shoreline hundreds of volunteers monitor sea turtle nests, document what they are seeing, and assist any endangered hatchlings that become disoriented in their quest to enter the sea and begin their lives successfully.

One such organization of volunteers is a group called Sea Turtle Oversight Protection (STOP) in Broward County. In 2012 this organization documented more than twenty thousand hatchlings that needed and received their assistance.

As the *Sarasota Herald-Tribune* has pointed out, "These sea turtles need dark, natural shores to nest and hatch" during the nesting season from May 1 to October 31 each year. The newspaper went on to note that artificial light, even the glare from street lamps, can draw hatchlings away from the water. This light pollution, plus noise, predators, and even the presence of beach chairs can fatally hamper the little turtles and prevent them from beginning their lives at sea, where they at least have a chance of survival. Turtle advocates and other volunteers help give endangered sea turtles a safer start, and thus offer some hope for the survival of these animals.

Other places where sea turtles may be seen from land include the following.

- Gumbo Limbo Nature Center, Boca Raton
- Sea Turtle Preservation Society, Brevard County
- Loggerhead Marine Life Center, Juno Beach
- Clearwater Marine Aquarium, Clearwater
- Mote Marine Laboratory and Aquarium, Sarasota
- Miami Seaquarium, Miami
- Sea World, Orlando

## Leatherback Sea Turtle, *Dermochelys coriacea*

Habitat: coral reefs, bays, and estuaries.

Size: up to 7 feet, 1,000–2,000 pounds or more.

Diet: carnivorous; mainly eats jellyfish, plus other soft-bodied invertebrates that float in the water, such as sea squirts.

Lifespan: 45 years, as estimated by *National Geographic*.

• • •

## Green Sea Turtle, *Chelonia mydas*

Habitat: tropical and subtropical coastal areas, shallow flats, and sea grass meadows.

Size: 3½–5 feet, up to 700 pounds.

Diet: juveniles are carnivorous, eating jellyfish and other soft-bodied animals. Adults are herbivorous (vegetarian), eating sea grass and algae.

Lifespan: up to 80 years.

• • •

## Loggerhead Sea Turtle, *Caretta caretta*

Habitat: bays, coral reefs, and river estuaries.

Size: 3 feet, 250–1,000 pounds.

Diet: carnivorous, eating lobster, shrimp, crabs, clams, conch, jellyfish.

Lifespan: 50 years.

• • •

### Hawksbill Sea Turtle, *Eretmochelys imbricata*

Habitat: coral reefs, rocky areas, lagoons, reefs, bays, and river estuaries.

Size: about 2–3¾ feet, 100–200 pounds.

Diet: omnivorous; mostly eats sponges, but also mollusks, algae, sea urchins, fish, and jellyfish.

Lifespan: 30–50 years, *National Geographic* estimate.

• • •

### Kemp's Ridley Sea Turtle, *Lepidochelys kempii*

Habitat: primarily found in shallow coastal Gulf of Mexico waters.

Size: 2–2½ feet, up to 100 pounds.

Diet: shellfish (crabs, shrimp), jellyfish, and some seaweed.

Lifespan: 50 years.

# Afterword

As must by now be abundantly clear, I love wildlife. I sincerely hope you have enjoyed sharing with me these encounters with some of Florida's animals and, that after reading this book, you have a much greater appreciation for and understanding of the wildlife with which we cohabit the Sunshine State.

Florida has been blessed with a rich diversity of wildlife. I've shared some of it with you on these pages, but there is much more to be seen. I can't urge you strongly enough to travel around the state and see these wondrous creatures for yourself.

Then, like me, I think you'll do whatever you can to preserve our wildlife and protect their habitats, so that continuing generations may also enjoy sharing nature's bounty and beauty in Florida. I hope so. The very important process of preserving our wildlife is endless. Perhaps you'll want to volunteer in some way to help protect and preserve our diverse wildlife. I strongly encourage you to share your talents as a volunteer.

I also hope that if you're a hunter, you'll change your ammunition to non-lead projectiles. And I hope you'll conscientiously avoid all use of those second-generation anticoagulant poisons that also are causing unintended wildlife deaths. Do these simple things for the animals, for your children, for your grandchildren, and for all successive generations—as your legacy to a biodiverse world.

# Resources

## Florida Wildlife Guidebooks

Ranging taxonomically from classes to individual species, books about Florida animals abound. Here are some general references to get you started.

Alden, Peter, Rick Cech, and Gil Nelson. *National Audubon Society Field Guide to Florida*. National Audubon Society Regional Field Guides. New York: Alfred A. Knopf, 1998.

Cerulean, Susan I., and Ann J. Morrow. *Florida Wildlife Viewing Guide*. Watchable Wildlife series. Guilford, Conn.: Falcon Press, 1993.

Gingerich, Jerry Lee. *Florida's Fabulous Mammals*. New York: World Publications, 1995.

Kavanagh, James. *The Nature of Florida: An Introduction to Familiar Plants, Animals, and Outstanding Natural Attractions*. 2nd ed. Waterford Field Guide. Dunedin: Waterford Press, 2010.

Maehr, David S., and Herbert W. Kale. *Florida's Birds: A Field Guide and Reference*. 2nd ed. Sarasota, Fla.: Pineapple, 2005.

National Audubon Society. *Field Guide to North American Birds, Eastern Region*. Rev. ed. New York: Alfred A. Knopf, 1994.

Sunquist, Fiona, Mel Sunquist, and Lee Beletsky. *Florida: Traveller's Wildlife Guides*. London: Academic Press, 2002.

Valentine, James. *Florida Magnificent Wilderness: State Lands, Parks, and Natural Areas*. Sarasota, Fla.: Pineapple, 2006.

## Florida Environmental Organizations

Here is an overview of some of the many wildlife preservation and land conservation groups focused on Florida. Most of them welcome support and volunteerism. A simple Internet search will reveal many Florida groups devoted to the preservation of particular animal species, such as panthers and manatees. Similarly, many regions and counties in Florida have their own land conservancies working to protect the wild lands that Florida animals need to survive. Be aware, too, that in addition to the Florida chapter of the Audubon Society, some areas host their own chapters. If you plan to support a specific group and want to know how your money is being spent, evaluate it through one of the sites that profile nonprofit groups, such as Charity Navigator (http://www.charitynavigator.org/) or Guide Star (http://www.guidestar.org/Home.aspx).

## Audubon Florida

Supporting their mission of conservation and education, the Audubon Society has a large footprint in Florida with twelve centers and sanctuaries and forty-four chapters throughout the Sunshine State.
http://fl.audubon.org

## Center for Biological Diversity

A national group, they use science, law, and creative media to protect the lands, waters, and climate that species need to survive. The group believes that the welfare of humans is deeply linked to nature—wild animals and plants.
http://www.biologicaldiversity.org

## Conservation Trust for Florida

This trust's objective is to protect Florida's rural landscapes, focusing on farms, ranches, working forests, and natural areas that provide landscape connections to maintain a statewide functional network of conservation lands.
http://www.conserveflorida.org/

## Defenders of Wildlife Florida

This national organization maintains an office and staff in St. Petersburg. From the Keys and the Everglades to the Panhandle, Florida is home to some of the nation's rarest places and wildlife, including some of its most imperiled species. Defenders is dedicated to keeping the state a wild and enchanting place while helping Floridians learn to live with wild animals.
http://defenders.org/florida

## Earthjustice Florida

Earthjustice is a nonprofit public interest law organization dedicated to protecting the magnificent places, natural resources, and wildlife of this earth and defending the right of all people to a healthy environment. Its purpose is to bring about far-reaching change by enforcing and strengthening environmental laws on behalf of hundreds of organizations and communities.
http://earthjustice.org/about/offices/florida

## Environment Florida

Focused exclusively on protecting Florida's air, water, and open spaces, this organization uses independent research and tough-minded advocacy to win concrete results for our environment.
http://www.environmentflorida.org/home

## Everglades Foundation

Dedicated to protecting and restoring the Everglades, this organization promotes scientifically sound and achievable solutions to reverse the damage inflicted on that ecosystem.
http://www.evergladesfoundation.org

## Florida Defenders of the Environment

This group has been protecting freshwater resources, promoting conservation of public lands, and providing quality environmental education since 1969.
http://fladefenders.org/

## Florida Fish and Wildlife Conservation Commission (FWC)

A governmental agency, FWC provides wildlife viewing and bear-proofing information on its Web site.
http://myfwc.com

## Florida Native Plant Society

The society's mission is to promote the preservation, conservation, and restoration of native plants and native plant communities of Florida.
http://www.fnps.org

## Florida Panther Society

This agency promotes protection and support of the Florida panther. It provides educational programs, coordinates public support of all Florida panther recovery programs, and supports reintroduction of the panther into presently unoccupied portions of the big cat's historic range.
http://www.panthersociety.org

## Florida Trail Association

The Florida Trail Association develops, maintains, protects, and promotes a network of hiking trails throughout the state, including the unique Florida National Scenic Trail. Together with partners the association provides opportunities for the public to hike, engage in outdoor recreation, participate in environmental education, and contribute to meaningful volunteer work.
http://www.floridatrail.org/

## Florida Wildlife Federation

Through education and advocacy, the Florida Wildlife Federation promotes the conservation, restoration, sound management, and ethical use of Florida's natural resources, so that present-day and future Floridians may live, work, and pursue outdoor activities in an outstanding natural environment.
http://www.fwfonline.org/

## Friends of the Florida Panther National Wildlife Refuge

A support organization of the Florida Panther National Wildlife Refuge, the Friends provide panther information and action alerts as well as volunteers to help keep the refuge panther-friendly and in its natural state.
http//www.floridapanther.org

## Nature Conservancy, Florida Chapter

The Nature Conservancy is a global organization dedicated to protecting the lands and waters on which the diversity of life depends. Its more than 1 million members have helped protect more than 15 million acres of habitat in the United States.
http://www.nature.org/ourinitiatives/regions/northamerica/unitedstates/florida/

## Save the Manatee Club

Singer-songwriter Jimmy Buffet and former U.S. senator and Florida governor Bob Graham founded this national nonprofit group in 1981 to prevent harm to manatees by human activities. It provides educational programs and helps fund research equipment and rescue and rehabilitation efforts. It also supports conservation and advocacy for Florida's official state marine mammal.
http://www.savethemanatee.org

## Sierra Club, Florida Chapter

Established by John Muir in 1892 on the notion that experiencing nature fosters a desire to protect it, Sierra Club provides wilderness experiences and opportunities for individuals from a variety of backgrounds to "explore, enjoy, and protect" the planet. The Florida chapter maintains an office in St. Petersburg and has sixteen regional groups around the state.
http://florida.sierraclub.org/

RECIPIENT OF THE SIERRA CLUB'S Ansel Adams Award and a Fellow of the Royal Photographic Society of Great Britain, Larry Allan is a writer and photographer specializing in the wildlife of North America. His photographs have illustrated many books and magazine articles. He is the author of a newspaper column about wildlife, a book on photography, and hundreds of magazine articles about photography, wildlife, and domestic animals. Allan also speaks frequently to various organizations and groups about these subjects, emphasizing his many and varied wildlife encounters and the urgent need to preserve wildlife and protect their habitats.

Additional photographs by Larry Allan may be seen and purchased at larry-allan.artistwebsites.com.

He may be contacted at Preserve.Our.Wildlife@gmail.com.

• • •